What would

Dani Do?

What would Dani Do?

DANI DYER

EBURY
PRESS

10 9 8 7 6 5 4 3 2

Ebury Press, an imprint of Ebury Publishing
20 Vauxhall Bridge Road
London SW1V 2SA

Ebury Press is part of the Penguin Random House group of companies
whose addresses can be found at global.penguinrandomhouse.com

Penguin
Random House
UK

Design by Emily Voller
Cover Design: Dave Brown
Editor: Michelle Warner
Production: Sian Pratley

First published by Ebury Press in 2019

www.penguin.co.uk

A CIP catalogue record for this book is available from the British Library

Hardback ISBN 9781529104264
Trade Paperback ISBN 9781529104271

Typeset in 11.75/20pt Bembo Std by Jouve (UK), Milton Keynes
Printed and bound in Great Britain by Clays Ltd, Elcograf S.p.A.

For Ariana – I love ya

Contents

Prologue

A BIT FROM ME TO YOU

Oh my God, I'm actually writing a book!

I never ever thought in a million years I'd have something that people wanted to *read*. When I was offered the chance to tell my story, my first thought was, 'Are you having a laugh?! What if people don't like it? And what do I say?!' But as anyone who's watched *Love Island* will know, I am never short of something to talk about, so I don't know why I was worried. It's so exciting to be able to put my words on a bit of paper and just be myself. When I'm asked questions in press interviews, I often feel like I'm holding a bit of me back because I'm scared I'll get caught out and something I've said will be turned into a mad headline; but now I can finally be me and tell you what I'm properly thinking about things. Nothing is off limits!

So, what is it I want to say? Me: Dani Charlotte Dyer, gob-almighty, who never climbs into bed without her trusty eye mask, has a weird habit of blow-drying her eyelashes and sometimes overindulges in cheese toasties . . . what on earth can I really offer the literary world? I'm not exactly Charles Dickens (even though I probably speak like a character from one of his books) or Judy Blume (she was my favourite author growing up – especially *Forever*; the one about the couple who had sex for the first time and the boy called his willy Ralph) or even Cheryl Tweedy for that matter (I loved her book; it made me laugh and cry loads) because she's a proper celeb! But despite only being 22 years old, I have lived a pretty eventful life. So, I want to share with you some of the things I've learnt and how I've come through bad times to become stronger, more self-confident and much more resilient. After winning *Love Island* (excuse me, but how the hell did that even happen?!), people often comment that I seem to really know my own mind; that I'm wiser than my years and that I seem to be a good judge of character. I guess

I've got some of that from my parents – Jo and Danny Dyer (or 'Big Dan' as he's known in our family) – but there's also stuff I've gone through myself that's forced me to develop a thick skin and understand how to cope with things like rejection and heartache.

When I was 16 years old, I wish someone had told me how to feel more self-assured, and the importance of making yourself happy rather than always trying to please other people (also, to never EVER let a boy control you!). So, I'm going to tell you how to deal with bullies, how to keep your chin up, value yourself and get that inner glow shining. And that, when it comes to friendships, it's really important to be a girls' girl and follow the girl code. Always back your mates no matter what. Your friends are for life, so you should stand by them – yes, it might sometimes get you in shit, but that's what friends are for.

My followers (I still can't say 'fans'; it makes me feel like I'm all up myself) are always asking for advice, so I got you to send me your questions on social media and I've tried to answer some of them as best I can throughout the book – so if that's you, look out for your name!

What Would Dani Do? isn't a normal autobiography or a memoir; instead I have decided to use your questions to help shape it into something I hope you will find useful. So in a way you have been my editors – thanks! I have listened to your comments and used my own experiences to answer your dilemmas, so I hope it's something you can relate to. One thing I was really struck by was how many of you asked me for the secret to being more confident because this is something I feel strongly about. We all deserve to feel like our best selves and be happy with who we are without comparing ourselves to anyone else. We all need to recognise that most of us feel unconfident at times and if we stood up for each other and supported each other a bit more then we would all feel a lot better! This book is a guide to getting on in life, making sure you stick up for yourself, not allowing others to manipulate you, and feeling good about how you look without thinking you have to change. By talking about certain things that have happened to me and the lessons I've learned, I hope it helps you in some way. But hopefully you will just enjoy reading it anyway – the ups and downs, the high points and the fuck-ups.

*

HOW WE FIRST MET

'Stay there, Dani, and the runner will come when we're ready for you.'

Prologue

I'm stood inside a little white tent. I'm sweating up. It's so hot in here. I'm wearing a one-shoulder strappy white bikini. Thank God I sent the producers three shit ones when they asked what I wanted to wear for my entrance. I bet all the other girls wanted to wear white but, somehow, I've managed to bag it! Tan's looking good. They've done my hair and make-up really lovely. I actually feel quite nice.

Fuck, I'm so nervous.

I need a wee.

And a poo.

Oh, why did I choose the white bikini? What if a bit of poo comes out? No one will pick me if I've got skids in my swimwear!

How long are they keeping me in here? It's boiling hot. My make-up's running now.

I feel so sick.

How long has it been now? *What? Three hours?!*

Can I have a can of Coke? I need sugar.

Maybe a beer too? Calm me nerves . . .

Oh no, what if I get belly bloat?

There's the runner. Oh, hello. You OK? This is it then. No going back now.

'Dani, we're ready for you now.'

They're putting a mic on me. 'Testing, testing one two three.' So, I've just got to walk to this car, and then I'll be driven into the villa? Arghhh!

I feel sick.

Here's the producer: 'When you drive towards the camera, stand up in the car and wave, then get out of the car and walk in.'

What if I fall out of the car while it's driving? I can't trust these heels. They make my legs look longer though. I need them to stop the stumps.

I'm getting really panicky.

'Dani, you'll be fine!'

I'm freaking out now. Why am I doing this to myself?

'Whoooo-hooo!' I'm in the car and I'm waving now, making my grand entrance. Looking like a loony.

My heart is about to fall out of my shoe.

I'm out of the car. Walking into the villa.

Feels like I'm floating and this isn't real . . .

This is either going to be the best or the worst thing that's ever happened to me.

Here goes.

'Dani Dyer – welcome to *Love Island*!'

*

ONE MORE THING . . .

My mum thinks people were surprised when they saw me on *Love Island,* because they probably expected a jumped-up-little-brat with a famous dad, who always got what she wanted. That's the reason she pushed me to go on the show in the first place. I really wasn't sure if it would be right for me and it took a fair bit of persuasion, but Mum was convinced I should do it, to show that I've got a 'good little personality'. I'm not so sure about that – personally, I think I'm a bit weird – but I'm so chuffed to be in in the position I am today, so if you voted for me, then a massive THANK YOU from the bottom of my heart.

Also, thank you for picking up a copy of my first ever book!

So here we go . . .

Let's get to know each other, shall we?

*

THINGS THAT ARE REALLY IMPORTANT TO ME

- *FRIENDSHIPS* – because you know your girls are there forever. They give you something different to a relationship and are always there to pick up the pieces when you're feeling down.

- *FUN* – laughter is the best medicine out there. You need to do stuff that's fun and makes you smile because that's what gives you your glow in life. And that's what will make you feel good from the inside out. Find at least one thing every day to make you laugh.

- *NORMALITY* – going to the coffee shop with your mates, having your nails done and a good gossip or getting pissed round your best friend's house. Hanging about with my real friends and remembering where I've come from.

- *CLEAN SKIN* – I am obsessed with keeping my skin clear because I used to suffer from bad breakouts and still get them when I'm stressed, so now I'm religious about how much I look after it. When I get out of the shower, I cream my whole body and then do my face. My mum thinks it takes me an hour 'creaming' but it only takes about 30 minutes.

· *CLEAN HOUSE* – when you have a clean living space, you have a clean and tidy mind. If my house is messy it stresses me right out.

· *KARMA* – think about how you act to others and always be kind. I really do believe that what you give out, you get back.

· *CANDLES* – they smell great and make everything seem so much nicer. I cannot stress enough the importance of candles. Just don't leave them too near your curtains unless you want to set fire to your house!

· *ARIANA GRANDE* – I love that girl. I don't know why but I just want her to be happy. I always think, 'I hope she's OK.'

SOME THINGS YOU MIGHT HEAR ME SAY

· 'I love ya'

· 'I've got the right 'ump'

· 'Let me give you a big cuddle'

· 'Come 'ere, babe!'

- 'Why haven't you folded the towel?!'

- 'He's made his cake' (I didn't realise the phrase is meant to be 'he's made his bed')

- 'Naaa, you're joking me, ain't ya?'

- 'Are you 'aving a laugh?'

- 'Spun me nut'

- 'RUDE'

THINGS THAT WIND ME UP

- *LAZINESS* – when people don't pick shit up for themselves because they can't be bothered to put it away or put it in the bin and always think, 'Oh, someone else will do it.' Well, why can't *you* be that someone else, eh?

- *TWO-FACED PEOPLE* – whenever someone slags their mate off to me, I think, 'Well, I'm definitely never confiding in you then!'

- *BUSES* – when they signal for ages and I'm in the car behind them. Are you coming over or not, mate? Because I really don't have time to sit behind you!

- *WHEN YOU'RE IN A BUSY CINEMA* and only two people are working there.

- *QUEUING UP* — I hate it.

- *WHEN PEOPLE ARE SLLLLLLLOOOOOOW.*

STUFF THAT MAKES ME SMILE

- *MY DAD WHEN HE WINDS ME UP.* He makes up stuff about what's happening on the TV and I always believe him. I'm really gullible!

- *JACK DOING SILLY WALKS AND ACCENTS.* He can literally imitate anyone he sees on TV and it cracks me up.

- *WHEN MY MAKE-UP'S BEEN DONE* (my eyeliner isn't wonky for once!) and I feel great about myself when I look in the mirror.

- *POSITIVE PEOPLE.*

- *THE OFFICE* – Ricky Gervais is incredible. I would have loved to have been in that show.

- *MY MUM* when she's made my bed for me.

- *MY NAN'S ROAST DINNERS* – they just mould together so well. All the vegetables are like mates on a plate, because she cooks them to perfection. You never have an issue like the broccoli being a bit too hard; everything just melts in your mouth.

- *MY NAN AND BRUV* – they make me so happy just thinking about them. I wish I could spend more time with them. They brought me up as much as my mum did, really, because Nan used to pick me up from school when Mum was working and she'd make me cheese and onion crisp sandwiches.

Chapter One

Are You Kidding?

Everyone says I was a funny little kid. For a start, I decided to call my mum's dad 'Bruv' instead of Grandad, because I really wanted a brother (which worked out well when I went to birthday parties – my friends' mums would give me an extra party bag to take back home to my 'Bruv'). And for some odd reason, I used to be obsessed with my nan's chin and I called it 'Chucky'. Whenever I saw her, I would grab the saggy bit of skin underneath and say, 'Look at that little chucky!' I was always joking about and saying silly things. I used to lock my great-nan (Nanny Julie) in the toilet every Sunday when we went to Nan and Bruv's for dinner because it made everyone laugh! Nan and Bruv had a dog called Dusty, and one day she got her tail caught on one of those sticky traps meant for catching mice, and I ran into the kitchen, wearing nothing but a nappy, shouting, 'Look everyone! Dusty's got a letter!' And once, I bought a selection of dog biscuits for Christmas and gave them to Bruv to eat without telling him they were for dogs.

I was very clumsy too. I accidentally put a fork in my mum's eye when I was in junior school and she had to go to hospital and wore a pirate patch for the next three weeks. Another time, Mum's dressing gown went up in flames like the kid from the Ready Brek advert because I didn't tell her I'd put the grill on stupidly high when she was standing by the cooker. Then, I set fire to the microwave trying to heat a leftover roast with tin foil on it. Oh, and I dropped Vimto all over my brand-new bedroom carpet just as the carpet fitter was pulling away from the drive. It was clean for all of five minutes!

I was also a right worrier. I worried about *everything*. When I was little, Mum says I would check the soles of my shoes in case they were dirty. I mean, they were shoes – of course they're going to be dirty! Apparently, I would sit and touch my hair obsessively too. And I'd panic about things, like whether we were going to get to places on time. I was a weird little child! I still have some silly quirks like that, like, I'm scared of tap water. Ever since I learnt about cholera in History at school, I have been convinced it's dangerous and don't drink it. I reckon that's the way the government will kill us all one day – through the taps! I also worry about old people. When I was younger, if we ever went to a restaurant and saw elderly people sitting, eating alone, I'd always make Mum invite them to sit with us at the table. It still makes me sad when I see an old person on their own now. I won't be able to eat my dinner unless I know they have company.

ALWAYS BE KIND TO OLD PEOPLE. HERE'S WHY:

1. People have probably died around them and they might be the only ones left. What if they don't have kids and grandkids to look after them?

2. Old people can actually die of heartache. Maybe your little twenty-minute conversation with them will make all the difference. I saw this little lady in Marks & Spencer the other day, and said, 'How are you? You look lovely,' and she replied, 'That's the nicest thing anyone has said to me. I haven't spoken to anyone today.'

3. You will be old one day!

4. They are cute. And they always have a nice manner about them. They never look cross!

15

5. When you get old, I feel as if you turn into a baby again. You have smaller portions of food and you can't do much or walk properly. And you wouldn't leave a baby alone in the street if you saw them, would you, eh?

What Would Dani Do?

♡

My parents have recently told me they're separating. What was it like for you when your parents weren't together?

My earliest memories are of living with my mum in her flat in Canning Town. We had a massive long corridor like in The Shining. *My mum and dad split for a while when I was about three and got back together when I was five. They were childhood sweethearts and had dated since they were 14, so it's fair enough that they needed to find out what life was like, snogging other people. Mum always jokes that Dad couldn't leave her alone and kept stalking her until she got back with him. I don't know how much I was affected by them living apart, but I think I probably pushed it to the back of my mind because I was so happy that they got back together! I'm naturally more of a daddy's girl than a mummy's girl, but I am now really close to my mum because of the time we spent together on our own. I think as long as you know your parents love you, then you will be fine. You just have to not let them use the fact that they aren't together against you – don't let them involve you in arguments or take sides. I never had time for any of that stuff.*

PROS AND CONS OF YOUR PARENTS NOT BEING TOGETHER

PRO: HOLIDAYS

Me and my mum were glued at the hip for the first few years of my life, and because she was young when she had me, we are more like best friends than mother and daughter. I was her little mate and she took me everywhere with her. We'd go on holidays all the time and she'd throw parties for me and the other kids in our block and would hire massive bouncy castles in the back garden. And whenever we were in the car together it felt like a mini road-trip because Mum would print the route out from the AA (we didn't have satnavs back then) and I would be the navigator and every point we reached, I would tick off, like I was doing the register.

PRO: LEARNING HOW TO STAND ON YOUR OWN TWO FEET

My mum was the breadwinner back then, and worked in the accounts department in Scotland Yard. She used to wear this crisp-clean white Ted Baker suit, and I remember she had another one from Austin Reed that cost about eight hundred quid (!); they were always dry-cleaned and she looked so smart and fancy. Although she doesn't work in an office nowadays, my mum is still a real grafter. She's also incredibly strong. She was a one-woman-show looking after me for a while, and never once begged my dad to come back to her. He might be the famous one, but she's the one who wears the trousers in that relationship. He can't survive without her. None of us can. She's the rock of the family; the one who keeps us together.

PRO: SHARING A BED

I loved nothing more than snuggling up in her bed. I slept with her almost every night. When she got back with my dad, I remember being annoyed that I had to sleep on my own again!

PRO: GETTING AN EXTENDED FAMILY

Because my mum had to go out and work when I was at a young age, it meant I got to spend loads of time with my nan and Bruv so we're a really close unit. I also got to hang out with my mum's neighbour, Sue, who I call 'Nanny Sue'. She always used to come on holiday with us, and I remember her babysitting for me and I would sit at the bottom of the cupboard eating Cheeselets until Mum came home. She loves singing and dancing too – I think she was one of the first people who taught me the words to songs. When I was

18 months I knew the words to 'Jimmy Mack' and 'My Boy Lollipop' off by heart (ask your nan!) and me and Sue would dance around the living room for hours.

CON: FIGHTS

I'm sure my mum had moments when she was sad about not being with my dad for those few years but she hid it well. She's not one to show her emotion through tears. She's more likely to show her feelings with actions. Like the time she threw an old VHS video tape at his head. Or when she cut up all his clothes or when she bashed one of his fancy cars in with a broom while me and him were watching in shock through the window (she ran around the corner to my nan's house with the broom after she'd bashed the car in, to fly off the handle – *literally* – about whatever he'd done to piss her off). I was too young to really know what they were rowing about but I remember moments. Another time she shoved a KFC chicken Zinger Burger in his eye. I thought it was a normal thing for your mum and dad to argue. But I knew they both loved me so I didn't ever feel too upset by it.

PRO: TREATS

Dad was away a lot with work, and he'll be the first to admit this was the period in time when he was partying like mad and going off the rails. He'll even say it's because he didn't have my mum to sort him out and get him on the straight and narrow! He was very young to be having a baby and didn't really know what he was doing. I don't think he really understood the concept of being a dad! But it also meant he felt guilty so he would buy me *everything*. He'd come over and see me on weekends and bring me little treats like this massive dressing-up box that had every single costume you could think of: Sleeping Beauty, Snow White, the lot. I loved girly stuff like that. That dressing-up box was the absolute bollocks. You could almost have an outfit for every day of the year.

PRO: TWO FOR ONE!

Most of the time it was just me and my mum, who was basically like both parents rolled into one. She is an amazing lady, my mum, and gives me serious 'woman goals'. We've definitely got our close bond because of some of our moments together when she was bringing me up. We still make sure we have our special mum and daughter dates and go for a nice meal and a catch-up.

CON: YOU NEED THEM BOTH FOR DIFFERENT THINGS

As I got older I would tell my dad I wanted him to come home. I missed his cuddles, his sense of humour and the way he read me stories.

Mum wanted Dad back too but she definitely didn't make it easy for him. Dad hadn't been great to my mum, so it took a long time for him to prove his worth to her again. He would come over to her flat and read me bedtime stories and gradually she would let him stay. I would look at him and say, 'Are you staying tonight, Daddy?' And he'd say,

'Yes, babe,' and would have tears in his eyes as he put me to bed. He told me recently it was everything he'd missed for so long. So that's how Mum and Dad got back together – very slowly until we were all living under the same roof and being a family again. Don't get me wrong, they'd still have arguments, but it was more over silly things like what was on telly (usually football) or whether he'd made the bed (he hadn't).

My nan and Bruv weren't happy about them getting back together though – they'd seen first-hand what Mum had gone through. They'd treated my dad like their own in the beginning – I think they'd even bought him his school uniform because he didn't have much money – but now he'd let their daughter down, so they weren't just going to let him back in the fold straight away. We'd go over to theirs on a Sunday for a roast dinner and for a while Dad had to stay at home on his own. But it soon became obvious my nan was softening, because she would make him some bubble (and squeak) and give it to Mum to take home in a doggy bag. They simply needed Dad to prove he wasn't going to mess us about again.

What Would Dani Do?

♡

Why did your dad give you the same name as him?

I think my dad thought it was funny! He was only 19 years old when he and my mum had me and it seemed like a cool idea at the time to give his daughter the exact same name as him. You'd probably say it couldn't get more Danny Dyer if it tried. The weird thing is, it was actually my mum Jo's idea. She says she did it, 'For psycho reasons,' just in case he ever got together with another woman and had a kid. She wanted to make sure she was the one to bag Dad's name first. I was nearly called Rosie at one point and then I was called Charlotte for about a week but that became my middle name instead. I never thought much about being called Dani Dyer like my dad until I started to do stuff in the public eye and had to explain that there were two of us and no, it wasn't a piss-take. Nowadays Dad just looks at me apologetically and says, 'I'm sorry about that, babe. I don't know what we were thinking.'

OTHER NAMES I'D HAVE CALLED MYSELF

1. I really like the name Elizabeth – you can be called Beth for short. It's got a bit of a royal twang about it and sounds fancy.

2. Otherwise I would be Effy – now that is a cool name. I loved her in *Skins*.

*

What Would Dani Do?

♡

My friend is being bullied but she doesn't want to tell anyone. Should I tell someone?

You definitely need to tell someone. That's what friends are for. Your friend might look at you and say, 'Why have you done that?', but ultimately that's what makes a friend. If you want to stop your friend being in pain and feeling like shit then it's your duty to help her. Friends are for life and you need to look out for each other.

I got really badly bullied in primary school. There were these six girls who did horrible things like lifting my skirt up in front of the boys. I used to put my knickers over the top of my tights as well as underneath them (I've never liked tights; they're really irritable and itchy and shouldn't be allowed near the Nunnie area). Anyway, one of the girls noticed. They flashed them in front of the rest of the class. They'd also do things like locking me in the school toilets and threatening to flush my head down the loo. They made my life absolute hell. My mum found nasty messages in my school bag that they'd hidden in there without me knowing – but she never told me what they said. I would spend every morning crying because I hated it so much. Mum was fuming and went to complain to the teachers. In the end, she was so angry she took matters into her own hands and went to one of the girl's houses and threw stones at her mum's windows. It wasn't the cleverest thing to do but Mum says she was so upset she *had* to do something. The girls did get expelled eventually. But Mum had the police called on her and had to face the school union. My mum was angry and upset, which probably didn't help me much, but that was her coping mechanism. That's just how she dealt with it. And I would act the same if my kid was being bullied; it's your natural reaction and defense.

I think it was my Maths teacher who put a stop to the bullying. He called the girls in question out in class and said he wouldn't stand for it. I can't remember his name but he was a big guy and he would always use digestive biscuits for the sums. I think he probably ate them all afterwards. He made me feel safe. I knew he had his eye on me, so people backed off. I don't know for sure what caused the bullying but I think it was probably jealousy because of who my dad was. My mates, and people we lived near, didn't care because they had known us all their lives but whenever I met anyone new, they would make assumptions and it could cause issues.

*

GOOD FOOD = GOOD MOOD

With Mum and Dad officially back together, we needed more space, so we moved from Mum's flat to a place in Custom House in Canning Town. I loved living there – we had a hot-pink kitchen and loads of fancy gadgets that my dad brought home. My mum threw out most of them because they weren't to her taste.

Dad worked away a lot, so I was still with my mum a big chunk of the time. Every Sunday evening, after the roast with Nan and Bruv, we'd go home and pick up a Chinese. By far the best Chinese in the world is Jade House in Canning Town; they used to give us these little carrier bags and I'd get chunky chips with barbecue sauce and special fried rice. We'd get home and watch a programme called *Dream*

Team and have a couple of bags of Discos. A lot of my best memories revolve around food. You always know what mood Mum is in by what she stocks in the fridge. If she's happy it's really colourful and the sight that greets you will make you think, 'Wow, I'm in the good books this morning.' But if you open the fridge and there's hardly anything in there you'll know you've done something wrong. Either that or she's gone on holiday.

FOOD THAT MEANS YOU'RE IN A GOOD MOOD: If my mum was in a good mood I would open the doors of the fridge and see a whole feast of different meats, my favourite chocolates, vegetables and beautiful salads like mozzarella and tomato. And she always has coleslaw.

If I was in a good mood and I wanted to fill the fridge for someone I'd make sure I listened really carefully to what they loved and surprise them. So for Jack, it would be anything snack-based:

1. Hummus and pitta bread

2. Feta cheese in cubes

3. Bags of assorted crisps (OK, they're not meant to go in the fridge but go with me)

4. Cocktail party sausages

5. Sausage rolls

6. Coconut pieces

7. Raspberries

8. Orange juice

9. Pineapple juice

10. Fizzy water

11. A big bottle of Coke

FOOD THAT MEANS YOU'RE IN A BAD MOOD:
If my mum had left nothing but a couple of cans of Coke and a pint of milk then I'd know she needs a nice cuddle because she's in a bad mood!

If I'm unhappy with Jack, I'll either leave him nothing at all or put a few empty cans of Coke in there just to wind him up (he does that himself without thinking sometimes!).

Talking of food, my dad fell asleep with a chicken once. A whole roast chicken that he took to bed with him because he was hungry but instead of having a plate, he dipped the chicken in salad cream and then he zonked out mid-mouthful with a leg in his hand. My mum woke up and was raging the next morning; 'There's a fucking chicken in the bed!' she was

shouting down the phone to my nan. 'Sorry, Jo, I couldn't help it,' Dad called down from upstairs.

THREE THINGS WORSE THAN A CHICKEN TO FALL ASLEEP WITH IN BED

1. *A KEBAB* – because you will never get rid of the smell of that stinky sauce.

2. *A COMPUTER* – I know someone who did that once and the lead was on her ankle and burnt a hole in her leg because the plug had heated up so much overnight!

29

3. *HAIR REMOVAL CREAM ON YOUR LIP* – I wasn't actually asleep when I did this, but I might as well have been, because I left it on for too long. It was the night of the TV Choice Awards, and I was in a panic because I thought I had a moustache. I didn't have time to go to the waxer's and get it done properly, so I got some hair removal cream instead – only I left the strip on for nearly ten minutes. As I ripped it off, my top lip started bleeding. I was shouting, 'Argh! My god! My lip!' Thankfully my make-up artist managed to cover it up but it was so sore all that night. I had to keep dabbing it with a tissue when no one was watching. Luckily you can't see it in any pictures!

What Would Dani Do?

♡

What is your biggest fear?

I'm so scared of lorries – they freak me out. I think they're too big for the road. I also hate gristle in meat, I don't like limescale and I hate gum disease, because I worked as a dental nurse so I've seen what it can do to people. Oh, and I hate cockroaches – you can't even tread on them because apparently they then lay loads of eggs on the spot!

'I've got a phobia of lorries – they freak me out. They're too big for the road'

I've been brought up with quite conflicting beliefs when it comes to little creatures and animals, because my mum and dad couldn't be more opposite in their opinions of them. Mum is very hard-nosed and would never go to the zoo. She will also scream, 'Kill it!', if she sees any sort of insect. But Dad is such a wuss he wouldn't hurt a fly. Definitely not a spider, anyway. He's convinced himself that spiders have family somewhere who would miss them if they died. 'What if someone squashes a male spider and his wife is sat in her web in the corner of the room wondering why he hasn't come home for his supper?' And he also sees spiders like his roommates. If I clock a spider on the ceiling he will say to me, 'There's no point in killing your roommate, is there? You should feel like you owe him something, you know?' I just laugh at him when he's like that. He's such an absolute idiot sometimes.

There was a frog in the living room once and my mum rang him up and made him come home from the pub. She was so scared of it and had never seen a frog before (why would you see frogs hanging about in the middle of a council estate?!) and kept screaming, 'Get rid of it!', while Dad was running around like a matador trying to catch it with a tea towel. I was petrified in case it hopped into my bedroom and it was jumping all over the place, slipping out of my dad's hands. He says he will never forget the feel of it because it was so slimy. But there was no way he was going to hurt it. I think it ended up hopping onto a bit of paper and he caught it with a glass and set it free.

We've had a few pets in our time, but unlike my dad, my mum has never been an animal lover. When she fell pregnant with my sister Sunnie, she decided to give our dog Treacle to Nan and Bruv, and my dad cried because he was so sad. But that was nothing compared to when we had to give our chihuahua, Dodger, back to his breeder. Dad was *properly* gutted. He really sobbed. It's still a bit of a sore subject, if I'm honest. I'd always wanted a chihuahua, but Dodger was different to other dogs. He was more like the runt of the litter. Dad has a knack of somehow getting lumbered with things that no one else wants. Dodger weed and pooed everywhere. I can smell it now! It was like Poomageddon. All because Dad had been feeding him ham during one of their evening bonding sessions in the lounge. How this tiny little dog could produce so much toilet, I will never know. Me and Mum just didn't get along with Dodger but my dad absolutely loved the creature. When we made him take him back to the breeder, he sat in the car and cried for hours. He was a broken man. He still won't forgive me for it now. Sometimes, when he wants to make me feel bad, he looks at me all deadpan and says, 'I proper cried in the car, I did, Dan.' The latest animal is a black cat he's adopted from next door. When I got home from *Love Island* I noticed it sitting staring at me from the back garden. 'Where's that cat come from?' I asked my mum. She sighed. 'It's your father – he keeps feeding it!'

While we were living in Canning Town, Dad landed a big role in *The Football Factory* and the money from films started coming in. He bought a Porsche, which he parked outside (he told my mum he'd got it for her instead of an Easter egg . . . but it was definitely more of a present for him than her!) and he would arrive home with all these mad things like bits of random art, a giant L-shaped sofa, and massive plasma TV that was so humungous you couldn't stick it on the wall. It took up the whole living room and people had to walk around it to get to the kitchen. I think you could even talk to it but it never understood Dad's accent so couldn't do anything he asked it to. Because Dad was getting more famous (that and the fancy car outside the front door), suddenly loads of people knew where we lived. Dad moaned our house had become like Stonehenge – 'It's the eighth wonder of the world!' – and said he couldn't even put the rubbish out without worrying there would be a pap nearby. We needed a new bin at one point so Dad had to try and hide the rubbish in our neighbours' bins. Imagine a picture of him prowling about like that! (Dad prides himself on taking the bins out because that's the only chore he does.)

We nearly got burgled a couple of times. Someone tried to nick my mum's handbag from the house while she was still at home! She came out of the kitchen and saw the burglar in the living room and somehow scared him off by shouting at him, but she says she will never forget his face. It wasn't until someone got shot down our road that Dad had had enough. He said, 'That's it now. I don't want to bring Dani up in this area.' He also reckons I was starting to speak like a rough 'un and kiss my teeth but I can't remember doing that! So it was decided we would move to Essex. That's when we moved to Debden.

The house in Debden was amazing. Our kitchen tap turned blue when cold water came through, purple when it was lukewarm and red when it was hot. And we had these beautiful bar stools with crystals round the bottom. But there were a couple of downsides:

1. My bedroom was haunted. I never saw any ghosts myself but it did have a really cold vibe about it and no one liked being in there. Danny-Boy Hatchard, who played

my dad's son in *EastEnders*, stayed over once after they'd been watching the boxing (I was out so dad told him to kip in my room) but he got so spooked that he left the house at 4 a.m.! He told me afterwards that he'd heard all these weird noises and got really freaked out.

2. I hated when I first moved to Essex. You might think someone like me would love a place like that – all the nice clothes and hair extensions – but back then I wasn't remotely interested. I had a rubbish layered hairdo and my idea of putting on foundation was getting a bit out of my bag on the way to school and rubbing it on my face, completely missing my neck and surrounding areas. So, to be surrounded by some girls who only seemed to care what they looked like was horrible. It was also a big jump from Canning Town. There, no one really had any money and it was just about hanging out with mates. I knew everyone around me, and we'd ride our bikes round the streets and just have a laugh. My nan and Bruv lived a VHS throw away, across the road. My other Nanny Christine was just around the corner and it was all lovely and homely.

I was 12 years old when we moved to Essex, and I cried nearly every night.

Chapter Two

Am I Normal?

If I could travel back in time to my teenage years, I'd make sure I'd stood up for myself more. I used to care far too much what people thought of me. My dad always says there are three things you should ask yourself when you're worried about something:

1. Is it going to be a stress?

2. Do you need to put energy into it?

3. Is it worth it?

If the answer to all three is, 'Yes', then do it. But if not, let it go. And he's right. I probably wasted a lot of my childhood worrying about pointless things.

I absolutely love Essex now, but when I started school, I really missed Canning Town. I was in year eight and it was the summer, so everyone already had their posse. It was like I'd stepped onto the set of *Mean Girls* and it felt really superficial and materialistic. Obviously not everyone was like that, but a lot of the the popular girls in my year wore Prada shoes, skirts up to their arses, had their hair dyed peroxide blonde and carried Hermès handbags. Back in Canning Town, no one gave a shit whether you owned a Louis Vuitton bag or whether you brushed your hair; it was about who you were, not what you had. And I wasn't that sort of girl. I rocked up on my first day with my skirt measuring to just-the-correct-length-it-needed-to-be, with a gigantic pink Nike rucksack on my back.

Everyone took the right piss.

I sobbed all the way home.

*

What Would Dani Do?

♡

I had an awful accident last year which meant I had to have metal pins put in my leg and girls at school make fun of me and tell me I won't be able to dance any more.

If you want to dance, then you should (as long as the doctor has said it's OK and safe). Don't ever stop something because other people have told you to. People are always going to be bullies and you will always come across mean spirits in life, but just try to tell yourself, they are that way because of their own insecurities. Besides, your metal pins will become your USP! Own it! Just think – when you go on a first date, it will be a talking point and a brilliant fact to show off about: 'I've got metal pins in my leg!' Yes, you had a terrible accident, and that must have been so horrible for you, but you are OK now. So, don't let it stop you from doing what you want to do.

I think the grief I got at my school was partly because of who my dad was. It was all very bitchy. The boys all loved the sort of films my dad was in, which probably made it worse for me because that meant they were interested in who I was, even though I wasn't very pretty. I was quite innocent and normal compared to the others, although I always ended up kissing the same boy on a trampoline. I remember hearing a girl behind us talking about what she did at the weekend; she was telling her mate about how she'd been touched up by a boy and I remember thinking, 'Fuck, where am I?'

What Would Dani Do?

♡

There's a boy I fancy at my college but so do loads of other girls. Should I bother going for it?

@shadenasinclair
Shadena, 19, London

It depends who the girls are. If they are your good friends, then I don't ever think you should let a boy come between you – it's not worth it. You should all decide to jog on and leave him to it, so nothing causes agg'. But if these girls aren't people you know very well, and he's giving you the signs he wants to be with you, then yes, go for it.

It happened to me with this boy in Essex. I finally kissed him at a house party. I was chuffed about it at the time, but looking back it was a pretty shit kiss, just a barrage of constant pecking. I hadn't kissed many boys so I didn't have much to go on. The first boy I ever kissed was in Canning Town a year earlier and that was horrible too. He gave me a sip of his Capri Sun and then took the straw out of my mouth and tongued me like a lizard. We were only 12 years old – who the hell knows how to kiss at that age? Anyway, back to the party. We'd had a few drinks and chatted a bit, then I had to go home early (Mum and Dad always made me leave places a good hour earlier than anyone else, which I thought was *so unfair*. If something ended at 11 p.m. they'd make me come home by 10 p.m.).

Turns out, once I'd left, he kissed one of the other girls from school. The next day, everyone turned against me because I'd kissed him. There was a clique of 'cool girls' and she was one of the ringleaders, so because she liked him as well, I was basically the enemy. I began getting all these abusive messages on Facebook calling me a 'slag'. And because we all had a BlackBerry, I was also getting BBM messages saying stuff like, 'What goes around comes around' – which at the time really upset me but, looking back on it, makes no sense! I mean, *what* comes around? But I just wanted it all to go away. There was only one girl who stuck by me, and that was my mate Liv. Without her I would have been lost. The boy in question didn't have a clue what everyone was saying, but I didn't talk to him again because I wanted to make everyone else happy more than I wanted to please myself. When I was 12 years old, all that drama made it feel like it was the end of the world. So much rivalry over one boy – it isn't worth it!

'So much rivalry over one boy – it isn't worth it!'

There was a song called 'Bulletproof' in the charts at the time and it would always be playing on the radio as I was in the car with Mum on the way to school. I listened to the words in an attempt to try and make myself feel a bit stronger, while bawling my eyes out as we drove towards the school gates. Gradually the tears became less and less until I'd stopped crying before we even got to Sainsbury's (which was about two minutes from my house).

But I never stood up for myself and I really regret that.

What Would Dani Do?

♡

How do you ignore the bullies and be confident?

@safalovekellieb
Safa, 19, Bradford

How can I be more confident?

@mary_mcbeth
Mary, 25, Bournemouth

Your friends might know your insecurities but don't show everyone your weaknesses. Keep some stuff back for yourself. As you grow older that's when your confidence comes and you realise you're not perfect, and that stuff you see in magazines isn't real. But it's hard to see that when you are growing up. But you really are different and unique; you have been put on this earth for a reason, and you shouldn't have to change yourself for anyone. Make your mind happy and fill it with good things because the glow a confident person has comes from the inside, not the outside.

'You get your glow from the inside – not from the outside'

ALWAYS STAND UP TO BULLIES

1. Remember that deep down the bullying person is just as much of a wimp as you. Bullies are all insecure – they are only putting you down to make themselves feel better.

2. Even though you might be shaking at the thought of it, if they say something to you, look them in the eye, and ask, 'What IS your problem?' Just confront them. Don't take it. Make it known that you have a backbone.

3. Know this: they won't be doing anything with their lives in the future. No one likes a bully so they will get their comeuppance.

What Would Dani Do?

♡

You always seemed so together on *Love Island* – have you ever got so drunk you regretted it?

@ivyrogg

Ivy, 18, London

The answer to that is a big . . . fat . . . YES! The first time I got really drunk, I was 13 years old. It was New Year's Eve and my mum and dad had gone to stay at their mates for the night. A few of us went round to our friend Megan's auntie's house and we sat swigging from a bottle of Jaeger, doing dares with each other. I decided to drink it while spinning around because it made you more drunk. Then I knocked over one of Megan's auntie's vases and broke it and proceeded to be sick all over the place. I was puking everywhere – Liv was trying to clean it with the mop and I was vomiting all over the mop head! The girls ended up having to strip me naked and put me in the bath and for some reason they also stuck sausage rolls all over me (I think they were trying to make me eat to soak up the alcohol). Liv was so worried she rang my mum and dad and said she thought I was dying so they made her put me in a

*taxi to their mate's house. I don't remember any of the
taxi journey but my mum said there were carrier bags
strewn around me because the driver was worried I
would be sick in his car. I was grounded for two weeks
after that.*

I really did love partying back when I was in my early teens.
These days I hardly drink because I hate the hangovers but back
then I would always be out on the town. Once I went out on
a Friday and woke up on Saturday on a building site! I don't
know how I got there; I'd been at a bar in Romford with my
mate Megan and we'd gone back to someone's pad for a party.
It was never anything bad and we weren't getting with any
fellas or anything; we just loved chatting to new people, getting
messy and keeping the party going. We weren't harming anyone
and nothing bad happened, but I know it was a stupid thing
to do. When I got home, Mum was doing her nut in. She and
Dad screamed at me, grounded me (for two weeks again) and
confiscated my BlackBerry. Every time I asked for my phone
back, they just added another day on. Even though Dad was
softer than Mum, he'd always stick to the same script as her
when telling me off. If he didn't, I'd hear them upstairs with
Mum shouting, 'You ain't backed me enough, Dan!'

One night, when Mum and Dad were invited out to
an event in London, I decided it would be a good idea to
invite twenty mates round. Big mistake. We thought we

were being really clever because we came up with the idea of covering up the security camera to the house so we could pretend it had broken. The camera was at the front door, which meant you could see who was turning up, so me and Liv devised a plan for her to place her school blazer over the camera – that way if Mum and Dad looked back at the footage they would just see blackout and we could pretend it had short-circuited. What I hadn't factored in was the fact that they would see Liv putting the coat over the camera in the first place! The event in London wasn't a late one so they were due back home at 11 p.m., which meant we only had about four hours to party anyway (so a lot of effort for nothing!). But we'd saved up most of our week's lunch money so we still had enough Glen's Vodka to get ourselves proper pissed.

By the time my mum and dad walked in, most of the others had been shoved out of the back door, so it was just me and a few of the girls left sitting on the settee pretending not to look squiffy-eyed. Dad came in and looked around; 'You alright? You had anyone round?' I tried not to slur my words. 'No, it's just been us.' What I didn't realise was that they'd already seen the evidence. One of the boys, Luke, had left some beer bottles on the front doorstep. It wasn't long before they checked out the security camera and saw Liv doing her blazer magic trick. We'd cut off the entire system, which meant nothing was working for months after that. So, I was grounded again.

Me and my mates used to think it was really cool to hang out in Camden but because my mum and dad wouldn't let us go into London, we'd tell them we were going to the cinema instead. I'd then have to watch the film trailer on the way home in case they grilled me about what the movie was like. I'd think I was the bollocks trotting around Camden in my yellow Juicy Couture tracksuit (for some odd reason, we'd put hairbands in the legs and rolled the bottoms underneath to make it look like they were shorter than they were) and I'd finish the look off with Adidas trainers, swigging from a bottle of Glen's Vodka. We'd just walk around, looking in the shops, wishing we could afford to buy something.

*

HEARTBREAK

What Would Dani Do?

♡

I have really fallen for this boy but I feel like I'm not good enough for him. Has that ever happened to you? What did you do?

I was 16 years old when I got my first serious boyfriend.

We dated for three years.

I lost all my confidence and ended up feeling like I was worthless.

Of course, it wasn't like that at the beginning. It was a gradual thing. But in the end I felt like everything I did in the relationship was surrounded by negativity and chipped away at my self-image until in the end there was nothing left.

I met him through a friend; I remember seeing him out in a club and then after I added him on Facebook he started messaging me. I'd never experienced love before so when I fell, I fell hard. He was a few years older than me and although he still lived with his parents, he had a job and he drove a car, which I obviously thought was majorly cool. He told me he loved me after we'd been together for six months and I was over the moon. He was my everything and for the first 12 months it was amazing and I adored him.

My family loved him too; they were happy because I was happy. I'd usually stay over at his house but he'd also be allowed to stay at mine. He was the first boy I'd had in my bedroom. I mean, my dad wasn't exactly shouting, 'Yeah! Go on mate! Get upstairs!' But I think both he and my mum knew they wouldn't see me much if they didn't let him come to our house. But they made me leave my bedroom door open so there was no way we could get up to anything anyway!

But slowly our relationship started to change. I felt like I was being judged – bit by bit I stopped going out with my friends and wearing certain clothes and make-up. Whenever I uploaded a picture of myself on Instagram I would get paranoid that he didn't like the way I looked any more. I found myself questioning everything I did and said. I tried to change myself so much that in the end I lost who I really was. I was so desperate for his approval that I would do anything to feel like I could please him. I was acting by this time, I had an agent and I was beginning to get some decent little film parts. I'd got my first role as one of the lead characters in a film called *We Still Kill the Old Way* and things were going really well for me. I was even appearing in newspaper articles – 'Danny Dyer's daughter is doing a movie' – and it felt sick, like I was really doing something with my life. I'd grown up loving acting because of my dad and now it felt like it was my time to shine.

But half the time I had to lie to this guy about what I was doing in the films because I felt as if he was jealous. He was upset about one scene in particular. There's a moment when it seems as if my character is going to get raped because this boy's pinning her down and it gets to the point where it's about to happen but then someone else comes in. It's not physical in any way; it's more about leaving the viewer with the idea of it. And to be honest it shouldn't matter even if it did happen because it's acting – it's a craft and a job. But he found it really difficult and it made me question the job I was doing. It made me feel so ashamed, when really I should have been loving the amazing opportunity I had been given. Looking back, we were very young and he was probably insecure, but at the time I just thought I was always in the wrong and that acting was one big mistake. I didn't dare tell my mum and dad that we were arguing because they'd have turned on him. My friends could see the relationship wasn't working and they would tell me they thought he was too possesive and wasn't right for me, but I wouldn't listen and slowly I saw less and less of them until I literally had no one left.

His unease got inside my head so badly that I genuinely thought acting was a bad thing for me to be doing. It was getting to the point where I'd go into auditions with such a face on me that I was beginning to fail. I wasn't getting offered the same roles as before. I was so down on myself, I had no confidence and started to think this was a bad career. So, the producers probably thought I never wanted it enough. I'd appeared in a couple of other films but after that I'd lost my oomph. My boyfriend was in the background saying, 'Look, you're not getting the parts . . . so why do you want to be an actress?' So, one day I rang my agent and said, 'Listen, I can't do this any more, it's just not for me.' I told him I didn't want to be represented and that he should take me off his books and stop putting me up for auditions. He was really shocked and rang up a friend of mine, another actor called Sam Strike, who played Johnny, one of my dad's sons in *EastEnders*, because Sam was also on his books. Sam immediately called my dad: 'Dani doesn't want be an actress any more?! What is going on?'

I remember walking through my door and saw Mum and Dad sitting, stony-faced, waiting for me. Dad looked me right in the eyes, 'So that's it? No more acting?' They both knew how passionately I'd wanted to perform – I'd danced since I was young, I'd helped my dad learn lines from his films . . . it was in my blood. I made up some stupid excuse about the fact that it just wasn't working any more. My dad just sat there and laughed at me but I knew he was sad, I could see it in his face. 'You've thrown your career down the drain, you've thrown it away!' he said. He's told me since that he was heartbroken and cried about it to my mum afterwards. He couldn't believe what I'd done and it affected our relationship so much that we didn't talk for a little while. I was on the defensive because I knew in my heart that I'd made a mistake and I didn't dare tell anyone I'd thrown this all away for a boy. I was so secretive about what I was feeling and what was going on in my relationship behind the scenes, I didn't talk about it to anyone, because I knew what they would say.

Deep down I think they knew something was up because my personality was slowly ebbing away and I was being really quiet and secretive. Mum said, 'You're not wearing make-up any more, Dan. You're not you any more, you're not going out with your friends, you're not doing anything . . . now you've thrown your career down the toilet?' Neither she nor my dad could believe it.

The whole thing with this boy became really, really toxic. We argued badly all the time and one of us would always end in tears. I hated him because I'd given up something I loved for him. We went on a couple of holidays together – one in

Amsterdam and another in Paris – and had blazing rows in the middle of the street. He couldn't understand what the problem was; he had literally no idea. He just kept telling me no one would ever love me like he loved me.

My 18th birthday should have been a really exciting milestone but it was shit. We'd gone out for a family dinner with my mum and dad, Nan and Bruv and he'd just had his head on the table because he'd felt hungover. Then he'd whisper little things in my ear like, 'I don't wanna be here.' At one point my dad had come over, grinning, and said, 'Here's your ID. So where are we going tonight, girl? We going to Faces?' He was bantering about taking us all to a nightclub in Essex now that I was finally legal to drink. Mum and Dad knew nothing about our problems, so despite his head being glued to the table, they still liked him. But after my dad mentioned going to Faces he mouthed to me, 'We ain't going there.'

What Would Dani Do?

Have you ever been to therapy?

Sian, 23, Windsor

Mum started to get really worried about me because I wasn't myself. I wasn't really eating, I wasn't sleeping very well and I'd lost a lot of weight – I was 7 stone and really skinny. I had no motivation to do anything. Mum says she seriously thought I might take my own life at one point because I couldn't stop crying and was so miserable. I would just shut myself away and sit in my room and not talk to anyone for days. So, she made me go to the doctor's. They offered me anti-depressants and I took tablets for anxiety for about six months. But I didn't like being on pills; I felt a bit weird and wanted another way out. I wanted to talk to someone. I had been in such a long and emotional relationship and ended up feeling so damaged, like everything was all my fault. I knew my mum and my friends would only see things from my side (Mum would back me if I murdered someone!); so I needed to speak to a stranger who didn't know me, just to see whether I was going mad or if this relationship was as wrong for me as I felt it was.

I was given a therapist through the NHS and before I met her I was in a right panic – I'd convinced myself she wouldn't care about me and would just look at the clock the whole time. But as soon as I saw her I felt my whole body relax. She was a beautiful lady who had a real warmth about her; she was a black woman with really dark short hair and held herself in a really smart and stylish manner.

When you see a therapist, they ask you some weird questions at first, all standard stuff that has to be covered in their questionnaire, like, 'How are you feeling?', and then, 'Have you had suicidal thoughts?' I wanted to hurt myself but I wasn't about to finish things off, although my mum said afterwards that she was genuinely worried I was on the verge of taking my own life because I loved this guy so much and she couldn't do anything to shake me out of it. I had ten therapy sessions and I didn't tell any of my friends where I was going, not because I felt ashamed about it; I just wanted to keep it personal to me.

My therapist was amazing and I can't even explain how much she helped me. I called her Jesus by the end of it because I thought she was so incredible. She never outright told me what to do, but she would just lead me to certain conclusions and make me see what was wrong for myself. When I told her about the fact that I'd dropped my acting agent for my boyfriend she just said, 'And do you think it's normal to have to give up your dreams in a relationship?', and I replied, 'No.' 'Exactly,' she nodded. Then she'd ask, 'If you want to wear make-up or want to dress a certain way why are you not doing that?' I cried virtually the whole time I was in those sessions with her but it helped me so much. Slowly she encouraged me to build up the strength to do something about it.

I was feeling shitter and shitter and I was losing all my mates. Then one Saturday morning, my best friend Kayleigh was at my house doing my nails for me. I had just eaten a bacon sandwich and my mum and my nan were in the kitchen. I really wasn't in a good place at all and, all of sudden, everything I'd been bottling up just erupted, and I broke down in tears. I sobbed, proper heart-wrenching sobs: 'I can't do it any more.' I was a crumpled mess on the table. I'd finally had enough. It actually makes me well up now just thinking about it all because I was so emotional and it was such a tough time. I was with this guy between the ages of 16 and 19 and they're supposed to be the best years where you have fun and crazy times with your mates. But the relationship took a big part of me away and I'm only just able to piece myself back together now. My mum and nan were crushed to see me like that. Nan says she was so hurt seeing me cry because I haven't sobbed that way in front of them before; I'd hidden it all inside me. They told me they'd do whatever they could to get me through it, and they did.

I'd tried to finish with him a few times before that but he would never have any of it. And I'd remind myself that I'd given up my acting career for him, so if we split up then what was the point? But this time was different. This time I had the strength. I picked up the phone and called him. He didn't even try to argue this time. I think he knew it wouldn't work. I was so done with this relationship – so, so done. But it still wasn't easy.

My mum slept with me every single night; she said she hated hearing her daughter cry herself to sleep. I was the skinniest I've ever been, I couldn't eat and I would mope about like a zombie but I knew I had to do it for my own state of mind. I'd lost myself, I didn't know who I was any more, I didn't know what made me laugh, I didn't know what I liked. I was poorly for about six months. One day Mum said, 'I really need to talk to you.' She told me she'd heard that my ex had slept with someone I knew just two weeks after we'd split up.

My mate Charlotte had told her because she hadn't known whether I could handle it or not. I felt absolutely violated. I couldn't believe it.

I still knew all his passwords so that night I tortured myself by reading all his messages and looking at what he was saying to this girl – which, of course, made the whole thing a million times worse. To me it was like he'd cheated on me because we'd been in a relationship for that long and then he got with someone else pretty much straight away!? I called him up, screaming, but he didn't get it. 'I'm not with you, so why does it matter?' The worst thing was that I'd shown him that he had the power to hurt me because I had rung him. My mum and dad were angry. 'What are you doing? You're ringing him up!' They knew it would set me back to square one again, back to the crying and the tears. After that they made me have no contact; they told me to block him from everything and banned me from looking at my phone. I was put on a healthy diet of spending time with my friends, family and people who loved me. And that was exactly where I needed to be. Then one day I woke up and I knew I was over him and I told myself I would never stay in the wrong relationship again.

I'd like to think I'm much tougher now. I know at 22 years old I'm still only young, but I've had a lot of life experiences and people say I'm quite mature for my age. Going through bad things like that can only make you stronger, I really do believe that. I also think that having to suffer heartache earlier on in life means it's never as bad again. It's like when you have chickenpox at a young age – it's just really itchy, but if you get it when you're an adult then it's fucking horrendous pain that makes you feel like you're going to die.

Of course, feeling stronger meant I would do anything I could to protect myself – which meant putting up barriers if I thought I was ever going to get hurt.

'Heartache is like chickenpox – if you have it when you're young it's just itchy but when you're older it's horrendous pain!'

A letter to my teenage self . . .

Dear me,

Please stop overthinking everything so much!

You are still so young and the worries you think you've got now will be insignificant by the time you grow up. Don't spend so much time stressing about what other people think of you and PLEASE stop crying so much over boys. Anything that seems so serious and important now will have vanished by the time you're older.

It might feel like everything is against you at the moment, but try to think of the fun stuff instead of taking life too seriously. Fun is more important than anything so laugh as much as you can. Try and start each day with a smile on your face. Be happy. Tell yourself, 'This is going to be a good day', and it probably will be.

I know you really feel like you want a boyfriend above all else at the moment, but please take a step back and think about why you want him and what he is actually doing for you. You need to think about yourself and what makes you happy; stop worrying so much about other people. Don't bottle stuff up – make sure you always talk about your feelings to others instead of hiding them away as they will only explode inside you otherwise.

Surround yourself with the people who make you feel good – not the ones who make you feel shit. When you're older you will learn that confidence – and your 'glow' – comes from understanding who you are a bit more, but right now you're looking to other people to tell you who you are and what you're worth – so make sure they are the right people! Spend more time with your friends and family – they're the ones who want you to do well.

While we're on the subject . . . have a bit more respect for your mum and dad and appreciate all the nice things they do for you. And when your dad takes you out to dinner when you're 16, don't look at your phone the whole time throughout the meal. He will be really upset afterwards and will tell you he felt like he was eating on his own. In fact, whatever you are doing in your life always try to find time to PUT YOUR PHONE DOWN. Don't sit in your room on your phone all the time – social media is a harsh place and never makes you feel good. Every time you go to pick up your phone to look at something think, 'What am I doing this for? What am I actually going to get out of it?', and go and do something else instead. Live your life in the real world, not the fake world.

Don't ever be embarrassed about who you are or where you've come from. You will love having a famous dad when you're older and he gets a lot of respect from people – there's a thing called Brexit which he seems to know more about than any of our policitians (and no, it's not a biscuit).

I know you got called 'Carrot Nose' by Frankie at school, but you will learn to accept it as something that's a unique part of you and makes you who you are. Besides, carrots are good for you – so that means your nose is too.

Please stop dying your hair blonde, it will break off like straw and you will look like a ratty mess and you will end up spending a fortune on extensions.

Keep doing your Coleen Rooney workout in your bedroom because it will keep you both fit and sane. It's not just about feeling better in your body, exercising helps your mind too. But please, when you fancy having a chocolate bar – just have one! Life's too short.

Stop stressing about the things you ain't good at – your art teacher was right, you just don't have the knack (you're never going to be the next Banksy!). So, instead focus on all the things you are good at, like drama. Concentrate your energy on stuff you love doing.

Do what you want to do. Be career-minded.

Think about your future.

And your love of shopping won't be a waste of time – you will be able to turn this into a career one day!

You shouldn't be ashamed of anything you enjoy doing. If you don't want to give up your Barbie dolls don't bin them yet! Keep sleeping in bed with your nan as much as you can. She is cute to cuddle and have chats with. Always make Bruv coffee in his special cup. And make sure you always keep your teeth clean because you don't want to get gum disease.

Love Dani x

dani dyer

Chapter Three

Family Values

You know when people say you can't choose your family? Well, if I had the choice, I would definitely have picked mine a thousand times over.

Ever since Dad appeared on BBC1's *Who Do You Think You Are?* and discovered that he has royal ancestry, we've all felt very special in the Dyer household. When the show came out, it made massive headlines in the newspapers because no one could believe that Danny Dyer was related to royalty. Dad was overwhelmed and couldn't stop talking about it. 'My great, great, great, great grandads are Kings of England!' he would laugh. And he wanted to make sure everyone knew it too. He got a giant picture of our family tree printed and framed for the house – with the royals at the top leading down to the bottom where my dad is – so it's the first thing you see when you come through the door.

I don't really understand it myself – I mean, how the hell are we connected to Edward III and William the Conqueror? – but I'm happy for Dad because it's a massive deal for him. He comes from a working-class family, so it's like he's now been accepted and can stick two fingers up to anyone who ever criticised him. At the end of 2018 we filmed *Danny Dyer's Right Royal Family*, which was hilarious because we had to dress up in the clobber they would have worn in those days and pretend we were Ye Olde Dyer Family. Me, Mum, my sister Sunnie and my brother Arty were in this big house and we had to stand and greet my dad when he came in, then we all had to walk through the gardens and dance, the way they would have danced. Dad was lapping it all up, putting on a silly posh voice and he had to wear an earring, so he looked like someone out of *Blackadder*. I was made to wear a stupidly tight dress; the corset was so painful and it had about ten layers. To think they had to wear that every single day? I couldn't breathe!

The Dyers are a really tight-knit bunch. We're a little bit nuts, but we're very kind with good hearts and we'll back each other through everything – good times and bad.

What Would Dani Do?

♡

Dear Dani, who do you take after more – your mum or dad?

@beau.dibbs
Beau, 20, Essex

I take after my mum and dad in different ways. They are both very unique characters so I'm quite glad I've taken a bit from each of them.

MY MUM:

My mum has so many sides to her character, you literally don't know who you're going to wake up to. Me and my dad call each other up to discuss who she is that day —almost to pre-warn each other in case she's in one of her bad personas.

Dad actually dedicated his wedding speech to the different sides to her character. They only got married a couple of years ago – after twenty-four years! – and Dad's speech was so emotional; he loves her so much he could barely keep the words together. But everyone was in stitches when he talked about her many personas and how he loves them all differently like Jo, Juanita and Ethel.

1. If you irritate or disrespect my mum then you get faced with Jo. You might get some dinner when you come home but you won't get any garnish. Jo will often blank you and not talk to you, which means you've done something to upset her. Usually this will be because you haven't seen her enough. All my mum wants from her family is their time; it's far more important to her than any material things.

2. Juanita, or 'Juana' for short, means 'Joanne' in Spanish. She doesn't appear for many people, just the people she truly loves. She's the really caring and thoughtful one. She listens, like *really* listens. I might mention I need to buy some more knickers, and then, the next day, there's a new pack of them in the drawer. She's always one step ahead of you. If I said that I had clothes in the dry-cleaners she will have already picked them up and they will be hanging in my wardrobe. Juana remembers everything and is so considerate and sweet. Even since I've not been living at home, she manages to surprise me with sweet stuff, like one day, I came home to the flat I shared with Jack, and there was a new pair of pyjamas on the bed with some chocolates and the sheets were all freshly made because she knew I'd been working so hard.

3. My mum says Ethel is a bitch but I think she speaks the hard, unvarnished truth! She doesn't come out much any more unless she's really needed. Like the time Mum had to talk some sense into me after I left *Survival of the Fittest* and was dithering about whether or not to accept a place on *Love Island*. I was telling my mum that I didn't want to do it because I just wanted to act. So, Ethel emerged and told me fair and square, 'You're not an actress, you're a fucking reality star!' It probably sounds very harsh when you read it in black and white – but it was said in a funny way and was meant to jolt me out of my wibbling rather than Mum truly meaning it. She knows I love acting and always will, but she could also see real potential in me doing something that showed my personality, and thought I needed a wake-up call.

4. Martha is really strict and will always make sure you're doing your homework or pulling your weight around the house. Mum says she has no choice but to have that many sides to her: 'I live with actors so I have to adjust to their performances!'

I haven't got *quite* that many personas. But I've definitely got some of Mum's traits. I get a bit of my snappiness from Jo, and Ethel has taught me how to pick people up when they're down. She will use tough love and do anything she can to jolt you out of it: 'What are you crying for? What are you doing?' There have been times when I've been sobbing my little heart out (usually about a boy) and she's sat outside my bedroom to make sure I was OK, but she wouldn't sit there encouraging me to 'have a good cry'. She would never show me how she's feeling herself. She might have a little weep in private afterwards but she wouldn't ever let me see. She always says, 'If two people are crying, that's twice the heartache. What good is that gonna do?!' So, I've learnt to do the same and make a joke out of it. When Laura was moping about over Wes in *Love Island*, I told her to stop sitting there fiddling with her lipstick and get back to being the Laura we loved again.

I've got my cleanliness from Juana – although I'm probably a bit fussier when it comes to making other people tidy up after themselves. I like to be in control of my living environment – don't ever get in the way of me and my mop and bucket. But until I started living with Jack, I never realised how small things – like, folding up a towel properly and putting it on the rail in the bathroom – could piss you off so much! He just chucks them on the floor when he's used them and it really, really grinds my gears. I mean, how do you *not know* how to fold a towel and put it on the towel rail??!

You might think I get my acting buzz from my dad, but my love of prancing about onstage comes from Mum too. A lot of people don't realise that she was a talented actress and singer back in the day. She wanted to be a pop star or in *Starlight Express* – she can really hold a tune – and is a brilliant dancer. But because she fell pregnant with me it meant she couldn't go to theatre school, so, in a way, she gave up everything for me.

MY DAD:

I've got my emotional, sensitive side from my dad. When I was five I had to sing 'You Are My Sunshine' in school assembly and I got so overwhelmed when I saw Dad in the audience that I started welling up. I was trying to hold it together but couldn't stop the tears coming, so he had to get up onstage with me and help me out. Then he started sobbing too!

If I really, really need a good cry, then I'll go to Dad. He'll lie there and hug me until I've let it all out. He's a really good cuddler. People probably think he's a bit of a wide-boy hard-nut but that couldn't be further from the truth. When we agreed to go on *Gogglebox* for Stand Up to Cancer, my dad knew he would be welling up on the settee. Mum always clocks him, watching TV and sobbing, and laughs, 'What are you crying for, Mick?' (she calls him Mick after his character in *EastEnders*).

Dad is a real joker and there's a lot of laughter in our house, which is where I get my sense of humour. Dad makes digs about Mum being too hard-faced and pretends he's constantly battling to try to make her more happy and positive. I remember once, we were lying on the sofa while Mum had this massive pile of ironing in front of her and she was moaning, 'I'm just the caretaker in here!' Then Dad beckoned her towards him with his hands; 'Jo, I'm really trying to pull you into the light but I just can't pull you in, you just won't take my hand.' And she clapped back, 'Well, I'm too busy fucking ironing!' (Mum is always ironing. She irons everything: bedsheets, jeans and even pyjamas because she says you have to go to bed with nice PJs on because 'anything can happen in the night'!)

One time, Mum and Dad came home from a date night – they'd been to an Indian and I was at home looking after my brother and sister – and Mum walked through the door with Dad following behind, his shirt open and his belt undone. I shouted, 'Oh my God! What have you two been doing? That's disgusting!' And Dad winked. 'She couldn't take her hands off me, Dani. She grabbed hold of me in the car.' I still don't know if it's true or not but they always do stuff like that just to wind me up, like snogging each other's face off whenever I come into the room.

I love singing too, which comes from my mum's side. As long as I've got my headphones on, then I will happily clean the house for hours and sing at the top of my voice. It makes me really happy and calm. Dad also has a good set of pipes on him. We are always belting out Ariana Grande songs. He pretends the steering wheel is a drum, and we drive around warbling away to her tunes at the top of our voices.

Dad sings to Mum all the time; he walks up the stairs singing old love songs. He's not a very confident singer in public but he's actually really talented. He was meant to play Bill Sykes in the West End theatre production of *Oliver!* but he slagged off the Nancys and lost the part. They were auditioning on that BBC1 show with Graham Norton and Andrew Lloyd Webber called *I'd Do Anything* and Dad was collared by a journalist at a party who was recording the conversation without him knowing. He said, 'I don't fancy any of those Nancys; they're all rubbish. It's more like "I'll do anything to be on TV".' It would actually be quite funny if it hadn't cost him the job. Dad never quite knows when to keep his mouth shut and he's *far* too honest with people. But I think the people who printed that story were really out of order. He had learnt the whole script and was about to start rehearsals when it happened, so he was really gutted. I went to see the show afterwards with my mum and although I loved it, I definitely think Dad would have made a great Bill Sykes.

We are also all fiercely protective of each other and always have each other's backs. That's a value of mine that carries through to friendships too. I will fight for my friends if I think they need my help. Once I'm mates with you, I'm with you for life, and will do anything to support you.

STUFF I'VE LEARNT FROM MY MUM

· Don't just believe in yourself – *love yourself*

· Do cute things for people to show you care

· Always tell the truth

· How to clean the kitchen really well

· Be confident

· Treat others how you want to be treated

· What you put into life is what you get out

· Don't be lazy

STUFF I'VE LEARNT FROM MY DAD

· Always be kind and think before you speak

· Be funny

· Never give in to anyone

· Put yourself first

· Never let anyone control you

· Be career-minded

· Enjoy your food – especially sushi

Then there's the rest of my family . . .

My sister, Sunnie, is 11 years old and she's the most beautiful and talented little soul. She's feeling really good at the moment because her big sister won *Love Island* and that gives her serious creds in school. She's only recently had to start wearing a tie to school and looks really grown up. Dad was moaning because he had to research how to do a tie up on YouTube. 'Dani, it was fucking hard, it was!' he said. 'You didn't have to wear ties when you were at school – is that a new thing?!' There's no doubt that Sunnie is going to do very well in life. She is so good with words, she can write so eloquently about how she's feeling. She's also brilliant at poetry and is always penning a little ditty about something or other. She's decided to write one for me just for this book:

My Sister Dani

It's OK to cry
I heard my mum say
Maybe not now
But you will be OK

What Would Dani Do?

Leave me alone, I'm alright
She says
She's brave as a ball
It's just one of those days

She will bounce back
She's Leo the lion
As tough
as wrought iron

Soon you will see
A bright smile on her face,
as quick as could be

She's funny, charming
Witty and mad
Very crazy and sometimes
Sad

She's sweet as a rose
And is shy with her pose
On Friday nights
She likes to dine
Drinking cocktails
And, of course, red wine

Her crazy hair
Can be a mane

Family Values

Her make-up is ditty
It makes her more pretty

She hits the gym
When she has stress
She should clean her bedroom
Because it's a big pile of mess

My sister Dani is coming
Home today
Her bags go flying
This weekend she will stay

I'm glad it's not Sunday
When I look her in the eye
To give her a cuddle
And say goodbye

Films, music and we
Like to sing
Beautiful clothes and
Anything bling

It's OK to cry
You're not a loon
If you miss me
Just look at the moon

Isn't she clever? Brings a tear to my eye that does (she clearly thinks I cry all the time anyway!). She's got a real talent for drawing and acting too – she loves a bit of drama. She's at the age now where she's transitioning from a kid to a young girl so she's always saying things like, 'I've got nothing to wear!' I really feel it's important for me to be there for her to guide her. I don't want her waiting outside shops for someone to buy her vodka like I did. If she's going to a house party and is going to drink then I'd rather buy it for her. As bad as that sounds, if she's going to do it I'd rather know about it. I will drop her off and pick her up so I know where she is. Life was all a bit more innocent when I was her age – the only naughty thing we ever did was drinking – but now kids take drugs and I don't want her going down that route. She's far too precious for that. You all are.

Arty, my brother, is five years old and he's beyond funny. He's got so much character, he's like a mini version of my dad. When he was at nursery he just referred to it as 'Friends' and now he's at school, he's loving it. He's honestly so charming already. I've gone downstairs wearing a little bit of lipstick and he'll say, 'Oh Dani, you look so beautiful with that lipstick on.' He notices everything. He runs into the kitchen to see my mum and will shout, 'I love ya!' But he does it really aggressively! He's got such a funny personality. The other day, he'd been naughty, so I said to him, 'What have you done?' And he replied, 'How can you tell?' and I answered, 'Because you're sad.' He shrugged; 'Well, I guess I'm gonna have to start smiling more often then.' He went on a camping trip with my mum's mates recently and there was another little girl in the car who was the same age as Arty. She said to him, 'Why are you not sitting next to me?' and he turned and said, 'Listen, I need to sit by the window because I need some air.' He behaves like an angel when you take him out, but he can be a little pest around my mum and dad. Dad is convinced he has less authority over him than anyone else. He says, 'Your mum's like a magician – she gets him to do what he's told. I only have to turn my back and there's cornflakes hitting the ceiling!' Dad makes a real effort with the kids and always makes sure he finds the time to teach Arty stuff like how to ride a bike and plays silly games. He's around loads more on weekends these days. When he first started in *EastEnders* he worked non-stop so would just have to sleep during any days he had off because he was exhausted, but now he's done his time there he managed to get more of a break. He told the producers he needed family time so they wrote his character Mick into prison for a while!

Dad does really cute things to show his affection. He's really good at cutting shapes into food and has done stuff like that all our lives. He wrote 'Sunnie' in chips last week and she loved it. He might be a shirker when it comes to housework but he'll try and win us and my mum over by cooking. He does a lovely roast dinner, which goes down well, but Mum refuses to eat his spaghetti bolognaise because she's scared of mincemeat. I have inherited a hatred of it too (it's all that gristle!).

Obviously Arty isn't the only brother I have. Bruv is the first and the original. His real name is Tolo but ever since I told him I wanted a brother, we buy each other 'brother' and 'sister' cards for birthday and Christmas. We were both massive fans of Harry Potter and each had Harry Potter place mats at the dinner table. When Bruv had his car stolen a few years ago, he was really sad, but not because he'd lost the car – he was upset because in the boot was a Harry Potter lunchbox I'd given him as a present. Bruv is from Majorca so I spent loads of my school summer holidays with him and my nan out in Spain (until I was a teenager and decided I'd rather get pissed with my mates in Camden instead). I used to be really good at Spanish and could hold proper conversations with people but now all I can remember is *caca*, which means 'shit'.

It's a right little love story the way he and my Nanny Carol met each other. She was 16 years old, on a girls' holiday in Majorca when she saw him in a bar. He couldn't speak a word of English so his mate came over and translated. They had an innocent holiday romance and when she went back to England they would write letters for years with his mate translating his letters from Spanish into English for him. He eventually came over to the UK and they got married when they were 21. How cute is that? They're still really in love now. Me and my mum always joke that we can't phone them up on a Sunday afternoon because they are probably up to something in the house. They have always stayed true to each other and I look at them as a real example of proper, true, romance.

Isn't it funny that *Love Island* was filmed in the same place they fell in love?

I've always been really close to my nan. She's the sort of person who will always 'say it as it is', which is probably where I've got my honesty from. If I think something is shit or if I'm not happy, then I'll just say so, because otherwise it builds up until you say something much worse. And my nan's always been very good at looking at two sides to everything. She will never just agree with you because you're her family. She's also drummed into me that I need to be respectful to myself and respect others. She's one of the main reasons I would never have joined the 'Do Bits Society' on *Love Island*. She would have been mortified if she'd seen me doing anything rude with a boy on TV!

My mum has a brother called Tolo after Bruv's real name, which is Bartholomy. He's the reason I like fitness stuff because we often go on little bonding running sessions. He's taken me on half marathons with him and we've done a few Tough Mudders assault courses together. For some reason he calls me 'Chook'.

On my dad's side there's my auntie Kayleigh, his sister (not to be confused with my best friend, Kayleigh). She's properly nuts. Genuinely the funniest person I've ever met in my life. Her and her partner Matt have two kids – Frankie and Mattie – and she's taught her little girl Mattie to cross her arms and give people dirty looks. Kayleigh could have been a comedian because she can stand up and make the whole room belly laugh.

Dad's mum, Nanny Christine, is the cool one. She's the person I'd ring up and ask for sex advice, more so than my mum. She was the first person who told me about periods because I went to the toilet and I saw blood and I asked her what it was. She and my dad's dad, Tony, aren't together any more but they are still on good terms. We never used to see him much, but he's getting better these days. I think he's come to terms with the fact that he needs to spend more time with us. We always joked how he would never take his coat off so he could always make a quick exit. But recently he's been turning up without a coat on at all, which has us all in shock!

My dad takes after both of them: Nanny Christine for the kind and emotional side; and Grandad Tony for his charisma. My grandad is very funny and charming, which is probably why he managed to get away with behaving in the way he did.

Then there's Dad's brother Tony (see, naming your kids after you runs in the family!) and he's the complete opposite of my dad. They are similar in some ways, but he's an accountant and is very well spoken. I don't know how he is the only one in my family with a posh voice, but we go with it.

We have a family WhatsApp group where we take the mickey out of each other constantly. It's just me, my mum

Where my personality comes from...

HEAD
Sensitive & emotional
- DAD

Career driven
- DAD

EARS
Loves the sound
of laughter
- AUNTIE KAYLEIGH

MOUTH
Always blurts out
the truth
- NAN (& MUM)

Not half bad at
singing - MUM

HANDS
Expert at
cleaning the
kitchen - MUM

Good at batting
boys away if
they get too
familiar - NAN

ARMS
Good at cuddling
- DAD

STOMACH
Fear of mincemeat
and gristle - MUM

LEGS
Great running
skills
- UNCLE TOLO

FEET
Nifty little
dancer - MUM

and dad on there because my sister and brother are too young. Nan and Bruv aren't allowed to join on there because they're too rubbish with technology. I've lost count of the number of times my nan has asked me to update her phone.

Phones are banned from the dinner table in our house. If I did get my phone out during mealtimes, my mum wouldn't say anything there and then, but later on she'd say, 'We didn't really talk then, did we?' Dad's the same. He never used to sit round the dinner table when he was growing up, so he likes the fact we have our family time. We can sit for hours just chatting about our day and discussing things that are bothering us. Even after we've finished, one of us will usually say, 'Right . . . carry on for another ten minutes?'

What Would Dani Do?

♡

What's the thing you like doing best with family?

@lolasutherland
Lola, 18, London

My absolute favourite family time is Christmas Day (apart from the time I ate a whole jar of pickled onions on Christmas

Eve and Mum had to rub my back all night because I was so sick). I love it when it's just me, Mum, Dad, Arty and Sunnie. We have a Buck's Fizz by 10 a.m. (you're allowed anything at Christmas!) and listen to music and chat. Then we sit and watch the EastEnders special. My dad always lies about little bits that are coming up and I'm really gullible so I believe him. He told me his character Mick was having an affair with Ian Beale once and I fell for it! Dad finds it hilarious. When we eat dinner (prawn cocktail for starters, then roast with all the trimmings), we chat about what we've done this year and discuss what could have been better. We really dissect the whole year gone by. Usually I've just had a load of heartache and grief from boys and been rejected from auditions but this year I dominated most of the conversation because so much had happened to me. I absolutely love Christmas, we just eat and eat and eat all day and don't change out of our pyjamas.

I don't think I even brush my teeth.

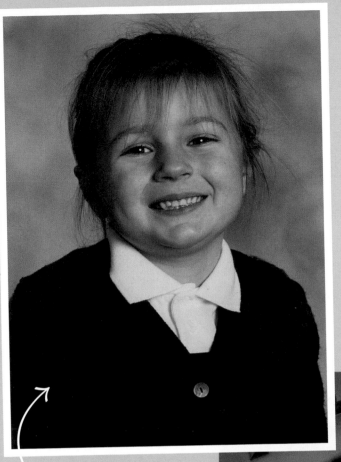

Such a
cheeky
grin!

Enjoying a bubble
bath - NOT a bath
bomb.

With my great-nanny Julie, who I locked in the toilet every Sunday! My face even looks like I'm plotting!

Forever a daddy's girl.

My love of make-up started at a young age!

Poor Dusty the dog didn't escape being styled by me!

Practising my moves.

Backstage at one of my early performances. Check out the leopard print.

Proudly showing off my new bike. I miss that house.

♡ x x

Enjoying some simple
pleasures with my dad.
Beer for him, pizza for me.

The family back together.

I loved summer holidays with Nanny Carol and Bruv!

Ultimate fan girl moment meeting Niall and Liam with my mate Daisy.

Rocking the uniform one last time on my last day of school!

Going all-out Essex for my prom with Saffron (left) and Daisy (right).

Proud moment completing a half-marathon with my Uncle Tolo.

Feeling all emotional as the Maid of Honour at my parents' wedding.

Girly day with my beautiful sister Sunnie and our incredible mum.

These girls have been there for me through thick and thin and I'm so proud to call them my best friends.

DANI'S DOS AND DON'TS

✗ *DON'T* spit in the shower or on the street – it's absolutely revolting and isn't anything anyone needs to see. Jesus didn't tell you in the Bible to phlegm everywhere, did he? It's DIRTY.

✗ *DON'T* have your phone out at the dinner table. And don't have your phone out when someone's trying to have a conversation with you. It's rude.

✗ *DON'T* flirt with other people's boyfriends. And what I don't get is that girls have commented before when Jack's posted a picture of us both on Instagram and said, 'I love him so much I'm going to steal him.' When did that become OK? That's not girl code!

✓ *DO* have my dinner ready as soon as I've finished in the gym; I definitely get HANGRY.

✗ *DON'T* pretend you're engaged and put it on social media – I did that as a dare when I was hosting a show on Capital FM and I wish I hadn't because everyone keeps bringing it up all the time.

✗ *DON'T* enter the room before I've had my coffee.

✗ *DON'T* poo in front of your boyfriend. I do not see the need to let those boundaries down – EVER! Surely some things need to be sacred?!

✗ *DON'T* be sarcastic – I don't get sarcasm. I don't mind piss-taking but not when you're nasty and sarky. I don't get it.

✓ *DO* make sure you have plenty of hobbies. It's good for you. I always loved dancing when I was younger and now I love running. I think it helps the brain to keep you busy – kids need to come home from school and do stuff that's fun, not get on their iPad.

✗ *DON'T* waste your money. You never know where your next job is coming from so never take it for granted.

✓ *DO* sometimes put others before yourself.

✗ *DON'T* let your boyfriend talk you into buying a dog.

✓ *DO* have more wardrobe space than your boyfriend. He can get a shoe rack and you have the rails.

Chapter Four

When I Grow Up I Want To Be...

I don't have a CV but if I did it would read:

DANI CHARLOTTE DYER – CURRICULUM VITAE

Date of birth: 8 August 1996

Personal statement:

**Extremely talkative, great listener, very affectionate, fun and positive –
until she gets the 'ump**

Things likely to cause the 'ump: hangovers, lack of coffee in the morning, not cleaning your plate away after you have eaten, leaving empty cans of drink in the fridge, rudeness, liars, jealousy or bitterness, people who brag about stuff, tightness, people who look at others funny

Key skills:

Good hair – *always kept in nice condition
(apart from when she was on Love Island and
it went ginger in the sun)*

Good hands and feet – *always has painted toenails*

The best kitchen cleaner you will ever come across.
And very quick

Brilliant at folding towels

Always on time – there's no excuse for lateness;
it's very disrespectful

Extremely trustworthy

Makes a really good sausage and mash

Could cuddle all day

Qualifications:

Talented actress (but won't lie in real life)

Qualified dancer and pretty good at singing
(especially Dua Lipa or Ariana Grande at the top of her
voice while cleaning the kitchen)

Very good at blow-drying eyelashes

Can pull a pint in under five seconds

**Great working knowledge of the inside of
someone's mouth** (having been a dental assistant)

So basically, my ultimate job would be something that involved cuddling and cleaning!

*

What Would Dani Do?

♡

What film can you watch over and over again and never get bored of?

Stand by Me. *It's based on a group of four boys on the hunt to find a dead body. It's all about the friendship that lies between the boys and is about growing up. River Phoenix is in it and he died really young. He was so talented and so fit! I would definitely have done naughty stuff with him.*

Me and Dad also love a good horror and can spend all day quoting lines to each other from films like The Shining. *We love going to the cinema, just us two, snuggling up and getting frightened out of our skin. I don't really know why I do it because I properly shit myself. We watched* The Evil Dead *together and were sooo scared I couldn't sleep for days.*

I've had the acting bug for as long as I can remember. When I was around seven years old my dad was making a film called *The Business* so I stayed with him out in Marbella in Spain during the school holidays while he was shooting. I would hang about on set loads and to me this was just a normal life. Every time Dad got a new part in a play or film I would help him practise his lines by reading the other characters and I'd get really into it (later on, I especially liked pretending to be his daughter Nancy in *EastEnders*).

From a young age, I found it easy to go 'off book', which is what actors call rehearsing without the script in front of you. Dad wasn't keen on me pursuing it as a career at first because he knew what a harsh world it was — he was a child actor himself and said that rejection is much harder to take when you don't have the life experience to back you up. But I loved everything about his world, and being on set with him was like the best day out for me. It's also how we bonded. I was his little girl, and instead of him taking me to watch football with him I'd sit in his trailer and watch him work. And I'd get to meet all his cast mates on his film sets. Obviously, I didn't have a clue who any of them were because I was too young to watch the stuff they were in.

I must have been about ten or eleven when he was doing a film called *Outlaw* with a guy called Rupert Friend. Rupert was dating Keira Knightley at the time and she would come to visit him on set. But the lucky thing got lumbered with looking after me instead! She was really lovely and kept me entertained playing silly games while they were all working. There was a communal pool as part of the block all the actors were staying in so she took me swimming a couple of times. I remember saying to her in the pool, 'I don't like your name, I wanna call you Lola.' And she told me that was fine and she was perfectly happy with that. She became like my big sister for the duration of the filming. I'd love to bump into her again one day. I wonder if she remembers me? When

I got back home, my mum couldn't believe it. 'You do know who that is, Dani? It's Keira Knightley, for God's sake!'

I met Stephen Graham and Noel Clarke on the set of *Doghouse* – they're both such talented actors and I just lapped up watching them work. They were really sweet to me too and would look after me on set. I'd also sit in the make-up room and pretend I was working there – I loved getting my make-up done in the chair. I remember thinking, 'Is this even a job? This is fun!' The producers even got me a small part in the end of the movie – and I was dressed me up as a zombie for one of the last scenes. After that, I couldn't imagine doing anything else; it was like this burning passion inside me.

I loved watching different scenes in films and rewinding them so I could study the faces and movements of the actors. I would soak up how they mastered the actions and thought it was so clever how they could portray such emotion just through their eyes. I just buzzed on it and I wanted to do it.

'I was picked to play Mary two years in a row at school – that's no sheep, is it, eh?'

I've never been one to jump out of bed and say, 'Yay school!' But because of my interest in movies, I did enjoy Drama and English. And, I'm proud to say, I was picked to play Mary in the school nativity play TWO YEARS IN A ROW. That's when I knew I had a bit of a talent. I mean *Mary*?! That's no sheep, is it, eh?!

OTHER THINGS ABOUT ME AND SCHOOL

1. I got a fountain pen for having good handwriting in English. Oh my God, I loved that fountain pen.

2. I played Annie in the school play (which in my eyes is nearly as good as Mary but not quite. She didn't give birth to Jesus).

3. I loved R.E. I found it really interesting learning about different cultures and religions.

4. School dinners were great – until Jamie Oliver took my hot dogs away on a Friday. He suddenly started piping up about healthy living and then my burgers and hot dogs were no more!

5. I used to get told off for talking too much. My form tutor was the worst because she used to make us read before class started. I wanted to have a catch-up about what my mates had had for dinner or watched on TV the night

before but she took that away from me. It was like living in the Victorian days.

6. I loved playing spin the bottle when we had parties. It was the best way to get to kiss the boy you fancied at school without looking like you were doing anything wrong.

What Would Dani Do?

♡

Dani, you're saying you can help us with our problems, well can you do my science homework for me?

Ha ha, funny question. But I hated science so I'm the wrong person to ask!

I went to theatre school at weekends from the ages of two to fourteen. It was called O'Farrells Stage School and I was a really good little dancer. My mum always tells me I should never have given it up but I never wanted to go down the musical theatre route. I'm not a bad singer but it was the dance stuff I loved more – jazz, tap, ballet, modern. I'd get home and prance around the house. When I was nine, I auditioned to be one of the dancers in the stage adaptation of *Billy Elliot*. It was so nerve-wracking and when I didn't get the part I was beside myself. I cried all the way home. Mum bought me chunky chips and barbecue sauce to cheer me up, and I ate them with a plastic fork out of the container. Neither she nor my dad wanted me going for auditions for a few years after that.

Dad clearly saw something in me though, because a few years later he asked me to play a part in a film he was doing called *Vendetta*. It was a bit random and out of the blue because I was at college (I studied musical theatre for a year but then dropped out) and he rang me up the day before filming to say that the actress who had been due to play the part had pulled out – she was meant to do a scene where she's dragged out of a car, but she'd found out she was pregnant so now didn't want to do it. So, Dad said it was mine if I wanted it. 'Babe, I don't know if you fancy it but I've got this little role at the beginning of my film *Vendetta*?' Obviously, I did! I was on set the very next day and I was buzzing. My scene took up the whole morning, I soaked up every comment the director said, and I totally nailed my part. Dad was watching on the screen at the side and he loved it. He was shouting, 'Go on, girl!', after each take. He told me afterwards he was so proud of me and thought I had a raw talent.

I signed with an agent then landed my first proper film when I was 17, playing the lead in *We Still Kill the Old Way*.

Not counting *Love Island,* I can truly say it was the best experience of my life; it was my first real acting job, and I was really chuffed because it did really well for a British film. I remember coming home and Dad would be up waiting for me because he knew I would be buzzing from the adrenaline and unable to sleep, so we'd sit up and chat into the early hours about how my day had gone and what I'd learnt. I left college straight after that because it wasn't doing anything for me; this was where I wanted to be.

I might have a famous dad but I've always been taught the value of money. I'm not one of those kids who got handouts all the time. Don't get me wrong, if I was ever in a bad way, my mum and dad would help me out, and they never made me pay rent when I was living at home. But I knew if I wanted it, I had to earn it. And acting in bit parts, being pulled out of cars, definitely wasn't going to pay the bills.

I got my first job as a dental nurse when I was 17 years old. My mum's mate was a dentist and she said I could shadow her for a couple of weeks. I loved it straight away because it made me feel intelligent and really cool. So, I got myself a gig in Valley Dental Surgery in Buckhurst Hill and had to study for two years while I was working (it's full on; you have to learn everything the dentist knows because you're handing them all the tools and writing up all the notes afterwards). There's a part of me now that will always miss it because I made some real friends for life at that place. The manager, Laura, is like a second mum to me. And Georgia, the dentist, was brilliant too. I really enjoyed it there; I was earning good money and I didn't even mind looking in people's mouths. But I finally left when I was 20 because I needed time to go for auditions. Dental nursing isn't a job that you dip in and out of – you can't just nip off for an hour here and there – because it's against the law not to have a nurse in the practice. So, I got a job in a pub: The Owl, near mum and dad's house. And I've definitely developed more of a taste for gin since that time in my life because we used to drink after shifts. The girls behind the bar became like my second family; we'd have such a laugh. But I've never been so skint in my entire life. It was the shittest money ever!

REJECTION

What Would Dani Do?

♡

Dear Dani, I love acting and go to an amateur dramatics class every week but I've been for a

couple of auditions for proper jobs and keep getting knock-backs. How do you cope with rejection?

With rejection, it's always going to hurt but it just shows how passionate you are. Just keep going and once you get that role it will be the best feeling in the world. It does make you stronger, so pick yourself up and carry on going – never stop. And let's not forget that some of the most successful people have been rejected loads of times – J. K. Rowling took her Harry Potter books to about ten different publishers before someone signed her. And Ricky Gervais says his idea for The Office was rejected by several commissioners before it ended up on the BBC. And can you imagine a world without David Brent or Quidditch?!

Pulling pints in the evening meant my days were free to try for acting roles again. Only problem was, I didn't get offered any. With acting, when you get rejected, you properly get dumped on your arse. It's really hard not to get bitter and lose all confidence because you can come out of an audition and think you've done well then you hear those dreaded words, 'No, sorry, you didn't get the part', and it totally floors you. You start questioning yourself and asking, 'What am I doing wrong?' And thinking you have nothing left to give. I can take constructive criticism but when you're told things like, 'You don't look right', then it can do your head in. The worst rejection I ever felt was when I auditioned for a part in a National Youth Theatre play and I really, really wanted it. They told me to arrive in casual wear with minimal make-up. I stood waiting to go in and this other girl was in the queue and she was all done up to the nines and started staring at me as if I was dirt. She looked like she owned about five horses and had never had to lift a finger in her life, she was so up herself. She sneered down her nose at me: 'Are you off book, Dani?' Now, as far as I'm concerned, if you don't know the script off by heart, I don't see the point of going to the audition in the first place. My dad has taught me little techniques for remembering scripts, like always make sure you know the beginning and the end of the sentence and also really think about what it all means so you understand it inside out. I'd stayed up all night making sure I had learnt the lines so I replied, 'Of course I'm off book.' She rolled her eyes; 'Ooh, well, I've had five auditions this week so I haven't had the time myself.' I felt like saying, 'Thanks for that, what a really shit conversation', because I hadn't had an audition for months. Luckily, she didn't put me off and the audition went really well. It couldn't have gone better in fact. You know when you know you've pulled something out of the bag? Well, that was one of those moments. After I'd finished they were full of praise and I walked out of the room thinking, 'I've got this!' Only I hadn't. Turns out I didn't look old enough for the role and should have worn a bit more make-up. The producer really liked me, and so did the head of the theatre, but the decision came down to the writer, who was also in the room. He said he just didn't see the character looking like me and that was that. I felt crushed. I cried all the way home. When was I going to get a break?

Back then I had the worst luck ever.

I couldn't even catch a cold . . .

REDEMPTION

Then, in October 2017, I was messaged out of the blue on Instagram. It was a guy called Lewis, a casting producer who worked for the company who made *Love Island*. He told me they were doing a physical challenge show for ITV2 that pitted boys against girls: 'We'd love you to come in for a meeting'. I ignored the message to start with. I didn't want to do a reality show; it just wasn't me. My dad had always taught me that if you want to be an actor then this is not the way to get taken seriously. After all, anything can happen on reality TV, so your life is in the producer's hands to mess about with any way they choose.

Lewis kept messaging me so in the end I asked my dad what he thought. Surprisingly, he seemed to think it was OK – mainly because I'd told him it was about fitness and he knew I loved my sports. 'Go for it, Dan,' he told me. Mum didn't take much persuading – she loves that sort of TV and can't get enough of the Kardashians and thinks she's the UK version of Kris Jenner (my dad just takes the piss out of them and gets clips from the show and dubs over them with stupid voices while he's at work in his lunch break).

So, I went to meet Lewis, and he told me he'd seen I was into my fitness from Instagram and thought it would be a good fit for me. We had a chat and he asked if I was interested in coming in for a proper meeting with the producers. I didn't have anything to lose, so I went. I wasn't prepared for it to be three hours of being grilled about everything to do with my life, experiences, relationships – by the end they basically knew what my intestines looked like!

I didn't hear anything from them until January, by which point, I'd completely given up. I wasn't even particularly bothered, because I was just so used to rejection by now.

Then I got the phone call.

'We want you on the show.'

I couldn't believe it. It felt amazing. I rang my nan. 'I'm going to South Africa!'

Two weeks after that, I was on the plane. Off to sunny Johannesburg for three whole weeks. Everyone was so happy for me – 'You deserve a bit of luck, Dan!' My nan, especially, was over the moon. Finally, something good was happening to me. This was it. My big break.

After one day of filming I dislocated my shoulder coming down a slide.

When I'd said I needed a break, I hadn't meant it *literally*.

It was the worst pain I've ever experienced in my life and I would not wish that on my worst enemy. The pain was excruciating.

I'd been in the middle of one of the challenges and as I landed at the bottom of the slide I remember thinking, 'What is this pain in my arm?' I heard a crunch and I carried on trying to climb through the mud but my arm felt like it wasn't coming with me, it was dragging behind. I was grimacing in pain. 'Oh my God, my arm.' The other contestants couldn't tell how much I was hurting so were shouting, 'Come on, Dani, you can do it, you can do it!' But I couldn't do it. 'I can't move my arm!' I wailed. The producers took one look at it and they knew straight away. I've never broken anything in my life but I couldn't move my fingers – I thought I would have to have my arm amputated!

I was gutted.

It took about four hours to click my arm back into my shoulder socket after that and I was screaming my head off. I was put on morphine to knock me out.

Lewis came to see me in my hotel room and he was clearly upset too. 'I'm so sorry,' he said. If it had been any other reality show, I'd have been able to stay in, but this was called *Survival of the Fittest* so I didn't really qualify with a wobbly arm. Then he looked at me and winked. 'There's always *Love Island*!'

I laughed and told him to piss off. I'd just about broken my shoulder, I didn't want to show the world a broken heart too. I called my mum and I was absolutely sobbing. I'd finally been given the opportunity to do something great and it was taken out of my hands – well, my arm anyway.

The most annoying thing was the fact that I'd read a book called *The Secret* before I went on the show – it's meant to change your life and be all about positive thinking. It tells you that if you believe in yourself you get what you wish for. Well, I believed in myself at the top of that slide but instead I went arse over tit, didn't I? And I definitely hadn't wished for a broken shoulder! I wanted to message the woman who wrote it to ask for my money back.

'I believed in myself at the top of that slide but instead I went arse over tit, didn't I?'

All I wanted when I arrived back home was a massive cuddle from my dad. I fell into his arms crying and he stroked my head. 'It's OK, baby; there's a reason why this has happened.'

Turns out he was right.

HOW TO COPE WITH SITUATIONS YOU MIGHT FEEL UNCOMFORTABLE IN

1. Keep yourself active before any big event or audition so you're not lying there thinking about it too much. Do something like going for a run or another sort of workout because it will help you think of other stuff rather than lying in bed worrying.

2. If you're doing any kind of public speaking or having to stand up in front of people, don't let the nerves cover the person you are. If you make a mistake then try to own it and laugh about it. Let it go; you're more likely to be funnier being you than reading off a piece of paper.

3. If you're at a job interview or an audition then go into that room like it's yours. You need to ooze confidence on the outside even if it doesn't feel fully there on the inside.

Chapter Five

(Finding) Love Island

The morning after I flew back to the UK from *Survival of the* (not so) *Fittest,* I was asked to be a guest on *Good Morning Britain*. My shoulder was agony, but I didn't care because suddenly I was being asked to do interviews as me, Dani Dyer, not just 'Danny Dyer's daughter'. They grilled me about my injury and what had happened and right at the end they said, 'Now, there are rumours about you going on *Love Island*?' I put them straight immediately. 'No, it's not for me.' Where the hell had they got that from? Why were all the newspapers saying that I was being lined up? There was no way I was going to put myself and my shitty love life through the wringer in public! What did they think I was – mad? Why would I want to advertise how much bad luck I had? No way. Not in a million years. Not even entertaining it.

'Everyone seems to think I'm going on *Love Island*!' I told my mum afterwards. She just looked at me and smiled. 'I think you should consider it.'

I sat at home for days after that, watching *Pretty Little Liars,* feeling really sorry for myself. I wasn't working, I had no money, I couldn't exercise, I couldn't drive, I barely left the house part from to go to physio for my shoulder . . . I was miserable.

On the plus side, my Instagram followers had gone right up since appearing on *Survival of the Fittest*. A guy called Adam Sutherland from Profile Talent got in touch with me and told me he could see potential in me and was interested in working together. We met up and I really liked him, so I signed to him as my new agent. I felt like he believed in who I was, which was just what I needed. That's why he's still my agent today, because he was there way before *Love Island* happened and stuck with me from the beginning. He started to get me some little money makers through my Instagram, which basically meant advertising stuff for different brands. I needed to earn for myself – I was broke – and I didn't want to keep asking my dad to help me out. I got paid per post on social media but I refused to promote anything I didn't like or agree with. Looking back now, there's still one thing I wish I'd not done and that was advertising a brand of shakes that are supposed to help you lose weight. I only did one post then immediately told Adam I couldn't do any more – I felt like it was a bad thing to be pushing onto young people. I only wanted to promote stuff I believed in. I wasn't going to sit there with teeth whitening strips or a bottle of bronzer if that's not what I used myself. I never wanted to lie.

More rumours kept swirling about *Love Island*. Adam asked if I was interested and I told him I didn't want to put myself through it. He just replied, 'That's cool.' Then the producers from E4's *Celebs Go Dating* got in touch and asked me to go to an audition. They asked me loads of questions about who my type was, how I was in relationships and previous dating experiences. I didn't especially want a part on the show anyway because it was a bit like *Love Island*, all about airing your love life in public. Just maybe without the bedsheets involved. In the end, I wasn't famous enough, so I didn't get offered a part. I was so used to hearing 'no' that it didn't faze me anyway.

A few days later, my mum brought up the *Love Island* thing again.

'You need to think about it, Dani. What have you got to lose? What else are you really going to do? Do you want go back to just working in a pub? Where do you see yourself?'

Then my nan started chipping in. 'We think you should do it. You were made for TV.'

'But I'm an actress, I want to act not just be on TV for the sake of it,' I reasoned.

(That's when my mum – well, 'Ethel' anyway – started ranting, 'You're not an actress you're a reality TV star!')

I'd been back home for about two months when I got a message from Lewis from *Survival of the Fittest*. 'Hi, Dani, how are you? How's the physio going? Do you fancy going out for a bit of lunch?' I loved Lewis, and wanted to catch up with him, so it was a no-brainer. I also think I knew, deep down, that he wanted more than a chit-chat. We met at a restaurant in the lower part of The Mondrian Hotel, near the ITV studios, in central London. He was asking me all these questions about how I was getting on, whether my arm was hurting any more, what was I up to? Was I having fun? Then I laughed, 'Come on, what do you really want to ask me, Lewis? You've not taken me out for lunch to talk about this stuff. You could have done this in a phone call!' That's when he came out with it: 'Why don't you consider *Love Island*?' By that point I'd given it a bit more thought (and still had Ethel's words ringing in my ears). Maybe Mum was right; what did I have to lose? Lewis asked if I would go to a meeting with the exec producers of *Love Island*, Tom and Lauren, just to see what they had to say. This was on the Friday, and by Monday, me and my mum were back in The Mondrian, sitting opposite them both at a breakfast meeting. I remember I asked for scrambled eggs on toast and they said, 'Dani, you can have whatever you want.' So, I said, 'Alright, I'll have avocado with it then.'

They were really lovely and told me about the show and what they wanted from this year's *Love Island*. I was nervous and blurted out, 'I don't want to have sex on telly!' Lauren looked at me. 'You don't have to do anything you don't want to do, Dani. We just want to see your personality. We see a lot of potential in you, and we were so sad when you had to leave *Survival of the Fittest*. We feel like this is your time . . . your chance.' That's when something inside me clicked and I changed my mind. I thought, 'They're right. No one's going to pin me down and force me to do anything I don't want to do. Maybe I can have my summer there and get a good tan!'

That night, I said to my mum, 'I think I'm going to go on *Love Island*.' Then she replied, 'OK, so are you going to tell Daddy?' (When I'm talking about him I call him 'daddy' but when I see him it's 'papa' or 'pops'.) Argh! I didn't want to tell him I was going on *Love Island!* He would hate it. When the rumours first came out, he'd turned his nose up and said, 'You're not going on *that* are you?' I think the *EastEnders* bosses had even asked him about it as they weren't keen on their star performer having a daughter in a show like that. He'd never watched it himself, but he'd just heard people talking about it. He, like many other people, thought it was a trashy show (I was so happy afterwards when it won a BAFTA because that soon changed his tune!). But while my mum was telling me to, 'Go for it, have the summer of your life!', I couldn't get the disapproval of my dad's tone out of my mind and I was far too scared to tell him. I half considered pretending I was just going on holiday to Majorca, but I couldn't lie. He would never forgive me if I was deceitful. That's worse to him than anything. I had to say something. I was just so petrified that I was about to disappoint him.

BEST WAYS TO WIN OVER MY DAD

- *FOOD* – If you can't take him out for sushi then he loves anything my nan cooks. Or if you cut up a sandwich for him in a heart shape, he'll lap that up.

- *FOOTBALL* – He could talk for hours about West Ham.

- *MUSIC* – He loves Kasabian and Oasis.

- *FILMS* – His favourite actor is Jack Nicholson so he'll watch anything he's in. I think he can see a bit of himself in him somewhere. They both have a naughty streak!

I'M OFF!

I made sure my Nanny Carol was there when I did the deed. I didn't want Mum there, because Dad would know she'd automatically back me, but he really respects my nan, and I knew she would be a big help with my argument. Mum made sure she was out with her mates, leaving Nan to cook for me and Dad. I can remember exactly what we had too. It was steak, jacket potato and this lovely avocado salad for dinner.

She put it out on the table and we all sat down.

Dad was opposite me and made some comment about how tasty it looked.

I watched him take a mouthful of salad. Right, there's no point putting this off . . .

I cleared my throat.

'I'm going on *Love Island*.'

Not one for allowing a silence, Nan instantly piped up in my defense, just as I knew she would. 'Oh Dani, it must be a good show because everyone was buying those water bottles last year!'

Dad slowly put his knife and fork down and just gave me a look. Then, without saying a word, he got up from the table, went out to the garden and sparked up a cigarette. I looked across at my nan, who smiled warmly. I didn't know whether to finish eating my dinner or throw it away.

'It must be a good show because everyone was buying those water bottles last year!'

After what seemed like a lifetime, he came back inside.

'Why?'

'Because it could change my life. I want to go and have some fun.'

'*Really*, Dan? Do you *really* think showing your love life on TV, revealing all your insecurities, showing everyone how vulnerable you are, is going to be good for you?!'

Then my nan chipped in again. 'Danny, what does she have to lose? She deserves it, this could be really good for her! What else is she going to do all summer?!' Nan did all she could to fight my corner, she was great. But my dad couldn't get his head around it. He told me he was never going to agree with me and that was that. He wasn't the type of person to ever stop me from doing something but he definitely wanted me to know he wasn't happy. We didn't speak about it after that. In fact, we didn't speak at all until the day I left. I was really disappointed because I didn't want to let him down. I wanted him to be proud of his daughter like he was when he saw me acting. I got scared. I wanted to prove him wrong, but what if he was right and this was a huge mistake? Well, it was too late to back out now. I had already signed the contract and I was due to fly to Majorca in a week . . .

The day I left he helped me with my suitcases downstairs. He still wasn't speaking to me about the show, but he gave me a massive hug and said, 'Go and do what you've got to do.'

I'd been warned by producers not to get papped at the airport because if I did there was a chance I might not get on the show. Despite the rumours, nothing was ever confirmed and they liked to keep identities of the contestants all under wraps. It would be just my luck if I got papped and was sent packing.

I wasn't taking any chances. I got in the taxi with no make-up on, Adidas trainers, a tracksuit and a hat covering my hair so I looked like a boy. I was really hungover because I'd been out the night before with my three best mates – Kayleigh, Charlotte and Ellie – they knew all about it, but they wouldn't tell a soul. They were excited for me but they too were worried for me too because of my previous track record with men. But they said to me, 'If you're just you and show the great side of your personality, you'll absolutely smash it. Just don't get caught up with the wrong boys because then you will show that other silly side, the one that cries all the time and has massive insecurities – people don't want to watch her on their TV!'

*

Having somehow managed to avoid getting papped, I boarded a flight with a girl called Tara, who was assigned as my chaperone for the week leading up to the show filming. We clicked instantly and from that moment onwards I felt able to relax. We arrived at a secluded hotel and I was told I had to give her my phone as we weren't allowed any more contact with the outside world. Even though this meant I couldn't talk to my mum and dad, I loved it – I had a week of pure fun with no one to answer to, sunbathing and drinking cocktails, watching Netflix in bed and eating amazing food. Tara made me feel myself again and really built up my spirits. I think she thought I was nuts because I asked if I could sleep in bed with her every night because I didn't want to be on my own. I kept badgering her about who else was going on the show but she wouldn't give anything away. 'Do you think there's someone in there for me?' I asked her and she just smiled. Little did I know at the time, but she was the person who had scouted Jack to go on the show so she knew my Mr Right was on his way.

Hand on heart, I honestly didn't think I'd meet anyone on *Love Island*. I thought I'd go in there for a few hours and get voted out.

The morning came, and Tara took me to a hotel where I got my hair and make-up done. I loved how I looked; they put my hair up in a ponytail and my make-up was really natural. I couldn't eat anything because I was so nervous. I honestly thought I might faint at one point. Then we were put in a white tent for about three hours until I was called to go in. That was when I was filmed for my big entrance, waving out of the roof of a car. Then I walked through the villa with my heart in my bum.

My first thought was how big the place looked – it was huge. I'd seen it on TV last year but it was a whole different ballgame to finally be there in person. I was fourth of the girls to arrive, so Hayley, Samira and Kendall were already there and they looked lovely. I suddenly thought, 'What if the girls are horrible or don't like me? What am I doing?!' But straight away they made me feel at ease, especially Samira. Laura was next to walk in and she obviously looked incredible. But we were all so different, I couldn't work out how I would get picked amongst this lot.

MY PERFECT MAN

- Brilliant sense of humour – he has to make me laugh, and takes the piss in a funny way

- A good tan

- Knows his own style but doesn't try too hard

- Is always honest

- Gives me compliments and genuinely means them

- Is cheeky and charming but not cocky

- Fit but doesn't know it

- Doesn't take himself too seriously

- Nice big eyes. I like dark features on a boy

JACK THE LAD

The boys came in one by one – Niall, Wes then Alex – and none of them were my type. I eventually stepped forward for Eyal because he had such a beautiful face, but he took Hayley over me. He wasn't really the sort I usually go for, but I liked his hair and I knew I had to pick someone otherwise I would get mugged off. At that point, me and Samira both looked at each other as if to say, 'This is it!' because we were the only ones left and we needed to fancy whoever was coming down next – he was the last boy. And his name was Jack. When I first saw Jack I thought, 'Woah, look at those teeth.' He had the biggest grin and all I could see were these bright white sparkly gnashers. He was wearing a pair of Valentinos and an open shirt, and I instantly got the fear that he was a wrong 'un because he was exactly the usual type I go for. But somehow my feet stepped forward for him . . . so did Samira's. He said, 'I'll choose Dani, she's lovely', and grinned this massive wide smile at me. That's when I thought, 'Here he comes. Here he fucking comes . . .'

Ultimately, I just wanted someone who would make me laugh. I never fancy boys to start with because looks don't mean much to me on their own. I need a good personality to make me properly fall for someone. It's very hard to find a good-looking boy who's flirty and funny – you never really get the mixture. So, to have that in Jack made him seem too good to be true.

Being on *Love Island* is nuts because you're sat with this guy thinking, 'We're in a couple, which means I have to get into bed with you later and I don't even know your middle name!' But Jack made me laugh straight away and I knew we had the same sense of humour. Turns out we were both shitting ourselves anyway, because when I said, 'I'm really nervous', he said he felt the same. He said he felt self-conscious too; he was the only one without a six-pack but I genuinely preferred him that way. That's what made him real. We asked about each other's family and when I told him about my dad he acted like he didn't know, which I knew was a lie. Of course he knew! I found out later he'd been following me on Instagram since the start of the year! I can't complain though, because he was a very loyal follower and liked loads of my pictures.

What Would Dani Do?

Who took the longest to get ready in the villa?

@Sammy_Lyons
Sammy, 20, Croydon

Laura. I never knew exactly how long because we didn't have watches so didn't have any concept of time but she was always the last one to come down of a night!

MY FUNNIEST LOVE ISLAND MOMENTS

- FINDING OUT JACK SOLD PENS FOR A LIVING. I laughed, thinking he literally walked around with a box of pens in a suitcase and knocked on people's doors. I didn't realise he had his own office and was part of a big company. I found the whole subject really funny and it definitely broke the ice between us.

- THE FASHION SHOW THE BOYS DID – Jack was sashaying about with shorts and heels on and I was strangely impressed. He had really nice long legs!

- WHEN WE HAD TO LOOK AFTER OUR PRETEND BABIES – ours was called Kimmy. I loved that baby, it was nice to be able to hold something other than Jack. No one else seemed to care for their kids as well as me and Jack did though. Josh's baby lost his arm and then Alex tipped his baby out the pram when the boys were racing!

- ALEX SAYING 'DOGGY FASHION' INSTEAD OF 'DOGGY STYLE'.

- WHEN ALEXANDRA PUT HER HANDS DOWN ALEX'S PANTS – it really made me giggle.

- WHEN I FOUND OUT JACK USED TO HAVE A
  POSTER OF MY DAD'S FILM *THE BUSINESS* IN
  HIS BEDROOM.

The first night in the villa was painfully awkward.
I hated having to get into the same bed as Jack. I was over-
analysing everything, thinking, 'Please don't touch me . . . oh
my God, he's trying to cuddle me, he's going to try and spoon
me in a minute . . .' I don't think I could have slept further
apart from him if I'd tried. Poor fella. Thank God for the eye
mask – as soon as that went on, he got the message. He told
me at the end he actually grew to love that eye mask and he
wouldn't have done anything with me even if I'd tried. He
liked the fact we didn't join the 'Do Bits Society' – it meant
we had something held back, something private between us
for when we got out.

I'VE GOT A BOYFRIEND! x ♡ x

I told him from the start we weren't having sex in there. Not
happening, no way. He admitted when he first came in, that
he'd imagined he'd be switching couples and swapping beds a
lot but then he met me and it all changed. After three weeks,
he asked me to be his girlfriend. I'd been happy with the way
it was going and felt really safe in his company so I'd never

put any pressure on him to ask me. We'd had conversations about it though, and I'd told him that if he ever asked me, I'd want my hair to be all nice and washed, my nails painted and I'd need to be wearing a nice little dress. But that night my hair was in a bun and my nails were all chipped! My dress was alright to be fair, but not one I'd choose for such a momentous moment. When he asked me to go with him to the daybed, my first thought was, 'Is he going to dump me?' Because he looked so nervous and had sweat running all down his nose.

'I've been having a think and that . . .' he began.

Oh my God, what?! Stay calm, Dani!

Then he told me he didn't want to be with anyone else and that he had never felt this way about a girl before. It was such a beautiful speech and no boy had ever said such nice words to me before. He asked me to be his girlfriend and I was elated. Then everyone (who were clearly listening from across the garden) clapped and cheered as if we were royalty! I honestly felt more special than Meghan and Harry at that moment. I was so ready to be his girlfriend, even if my hair was shit.

What Would Dani Do?

♡

How much of *Love Island* is set up?

@beccatayloooor
Becca, 23, London

It's not set up; whatever conversation you want to have you have. They just have to have a bit of a structure to it because it is a reality show.

When you're in the villa, you do honestly forget about the cameras. Me and Jack had a big snog on one of the sofas and when I watched it back on TV afterwards it made me cringe. I thought the producers kept the camera on us for far too long – they should've edited that kiss right down! I actually timed how long we kissed for; it was three minutes! Why does anyone need to see that much snogging? Even though the cameras are hidden, the producers did still pop out into the villa every now and then to encourage certain conversations or ask us to hold off until they were ready. But I understood why. They had to make a TV show at the end of the day, so they wanted to spread out the drama, otherwise it would end at evening time and everyone would have said everything they needed to say to each other! Nothing was ever forced though – if you wanted to do or say something you wouldn't be encouraged to do anything different. And if you felt down, you'd be able to go and meet one of the producers at the side door and have a little chat and cuddle, or you could ask to see one the psychologists.

I didn't tell Jack I loved him until after Casa Amor. That was the part of the show when the boys were sent to a different villa for a few nights, where there were a load of other girls waiting to tempt them. About a day into their visit, we were sent a video of what they'd been up to and it floored me. There was a clip of Jack's reaction as the new girls came into their villa and the camera stuck on him as he looked completely shocked and could be seen mouthing, 'Oh my God, oh my God!' as he told the other boys that one of the girls was his ex!

To hear that a girl he'd been seeing before *Love Island* was now in a villa with him just brought all my past insecurities flooding back. I was in bits. I couldn't stop crying and I thought it was game over because there was no way Jack wouldn't get it on with her. I knew it was too good to be true. Bad things always happened to me and this was just proof that I was never destined to find love. Why did he keep saying, 'Oh my God!'? He said it one too many times as far as I was concerned. I went into the beach hut, mascara streaming down my face and I sobbed my heart out. My mind was racing . . . what is he doing? Is he happier with her? Is she prettier than me? Does she make him laugh?!!

I just wanted to go home. I was so worried I was going to mug myself off. But the producers got one of the psychologists to talk to me and they persuaded me to stay. I agreed on the condition that I would wait until Jack came back to the villa and if he returned with his ex then I would be on that first plane home. I was hurting so much. I felt sorry for Georgia too; she was panicking about what Josh was up to (he'd been caught out in another video). The boys were in Casa Amor for four days. I kept going to the beach hut and yelling, 'They've been in there long enough! They don't need another day!' On last year's show they were only in there for two days. Why were they torturing me like this!?

This was my worst nightmare. It was exactly what every one of my friends and family thought would happen. I'd let my dad down.

What was he going to say?

What I didn't realise was that back home, my dad was also in a state, because he was watching this all unfold on TV. All he could see was me in floods of tears while he watched the box helplessly, convinced I would be scarred for life.

Meanwhile, my mum was on the phone to the producers telling them they had to get me out of there!

My mum and dad nearly fell out over me going on *Love Island*. Dad had made no secret of the fact he didn't want me to do it, and he'd warned her, 'If this show fucks our child up, it's on your shoulders.' He was really worried that I would crumble in front of the cameras, and knew from experience how easily public opinion could turn on someone.

Mum says they often had to watch it in different rooms. They'd reconvene after each episode and Dad would say things like, 'She's doing alright, isn't she?' While Mum would say, 'Doesn't she look pretty in her bikini?'

But it was during the Casa Amor episodes that my dad went properly apeshit, because he thought I was about to have a breakdown. My mum had just landed in Ibiza – she was on a four-day break with one of her mates – when Dad called her up, ranting.

'Get her out now! She's crying, Jack's ex has come in!'

Mum had been on a flight so she didn't have a clue what he was on about. She had missed the episode where Jack was in Casa Amor and I had been shown the video footage of him saying his ex was in there.

'What's she crying for?' she asked him.

'She's going wonky!' he was shouting. 'Our child is going to crumble so you had better go over and get her!'

'But I've just got to Ibiza!'

'I'm telling you now, she's in bits! This is what I was worried about!'

My mum called all her mates, who sent her clips of me in tears in the beach hut. My nan was worried about me. Sunnie was in tears watching me. Everyone back home was fearful that I was losing it – because this was always what happened to me and boys. And they thought my anxiety was going to kick in again. I always seemed to be jinxed.

As far as my family and friends were all concerned, this whole thing with Jack had been far too good to be true.

So, my mum rang Lewis and made him put her through to the producers.

'I need to get Dani out of the show – NOW!'

Thank God, she called a few hours too late. The show is filmed ahead of it airing, so by the time she'd got through to the producers, the whole Casa Amor saga had ended and I was back on track with Jack.

'Listen, Jo, Dani is fine. It's all over and done with. She's OK now.'

Somehow, they managed to convince my mum to stay on her sunlounger.

LOVE IS IN THE AIR

The night Jack and the other boys were due back in our villa, I felt sick to my stomach. Despite feeling so shit and vulnerable there was never any doubt that I would still stick with Jack. I didn't want anyone else, I knew right there and then that I loved him. I had to take my chance and see if he felt the same or not. I made sure I dressed in an outfit that he would remember — it was sexier than I'd usually wear but I wanted him to notice me. I wore a little black thong leotard with a see-through dress over the top and a belt pinching my waist. My hair was washed and curled, and the girls had helped me do my eye make-up. I thought, 'If he comes back in with some angel at least I can leave looking like the Devil.'

Caroline Flack asked me if I was going to Stick or Twist. I stood up and my heart was jumping out of my chest. By this time some of the boys had already come back in, all with new girls on their arms. Adam was with a girl called Darylle and Dr Alex was with Grace. I tried to catch Alex's eye to see if he would give me a sign — just a wink, or a smile or something? But he couldn't look at me. I was thinking, 'Why can't you look me in the eye, Alex?!' I stared at Caroline but she wasn't giving anything away either.

'What are you going to do, Dani?'

I took a deep breath. I told myself, 'Please don't cry', but my voice was shaking. 'I'll stick with Jack.'

Caroline called for Jack to come through. 'Is he alone? Let's find out.'

I listened for the sound of footsteps. There was a hidden walkway behind us so we could hear them before we could see anyone and when Adam and Alex had come into the villa there had been the unmistakable sound of a girl's shoes clicking along the path, so we knew they hadn't been alone. I said to Georgia, 'I can't look, I can't look,' and took a deep breath. I couldn't hear anything . . . was he alone? I glanced at Samira, who mouthed, 'It's fine, Dan, it's fine,' and then I saw Jack grinning at me. I was so overcome with emotion. I wanted to blurt out there and then, 'I love you!' But at the same time wanted to punch him for putting me through so much heartache. He gave me a kiss and a hug and sat back down with me and I was so relieved. I couldn't stop touching his hands, I needed to check he was real!

My next thought was, 'Where's your ex? Is she coming in?' And then she came in with Sam (who'd joined us in the villa a few days before). I knew it was her, just from the way she looked. I knew she would be Jack's type – petite and pretty with brown hair. Her name was Ellie. Me and Samira gave each other a look to say, 'That's HER,' and I thought, 'Why is she even here? Can't she leave us alone?' I didn't want to talk to her, I didn't want to be near her. How could I be friends with his ex?

That night, in bed with Jack, I had to hold myself back from doing anything more than kissing. We'd been apart for what seemed like weeks, and I was so happy to be close to him again. I really fancied him and couldn't keep my hands off him. At one point, I had to have a word with myself. 'Dani, we're in the danger zone here!' So I turned away from him.

'Don't ever leave me again!' I whispered.

'Dan, I really like you.'

'I really like you too.'

'No, I really, *really* like you.'

I laughed and thought, 'Where are we going with this?!'

'I think I love you.'

'I love you too.'

I had the biggest grin on my face. I felt like a little girl.

The next day, it felt like Christmas morning. You know when you go downstairs and you don't know what presents you're going to open because there are just so many? It was just like that, and I was on top of the world.

*

What Would Dani Do?

♡

Did anyone have any accidents we didn't know about or have to go to the doctor?

@emilypackham
Emily, 23, Surrey

I had a kidney infection twice and had to go on a drip!

THE BIG TEST

The one time we did have a major fall out was after the lie detector test near the end of the show. Each girl had to write a list of questions they wanted their boy to be asked, and the lie detector would tell us if they were genuine or not. I wanted to know things like whether Jack thought we would get married, whether he loved me and whether we would work in the outside world. But my biggest stress was whether his head would be turned by other girls – I'd been cheated on and lied to in so many previous relationships that this was the main thing I was in a stress about.

He got strapped up to the machine, and was asked, 'Do you love Dani?', to which he replied, 'Yes', and it came up 'True'. I also wanted to know if he would like me a bit sexier and he said, 'No', which came up as a 'Lie' but I didn't mind that. Of course, he probably wants me to dress in something better than fluffy slippers in the bedroom! He was also asked, 'Did you couple up with Dani because you knew who her dad was?', which must've touched a nerve because he got a bit mad with that one. 'That's really annoyed me, that question. That's ridiculous – no!' But the machine came back saying that he was lying! He said he could see us married, which made me happy, but then it was time for the question I had most of my hopes pinned on. He was asked if his eyes would stray outside the villa and when he said, 'No', the detector said he was lying. I was so upset. I couldn't help myself. This was my worst fear. After that I just saw red. It felt like he'd already done something wrong and I got in a right hump with him. We had a blazing row because I was trying to explain that this was the thing I'd been most fearful of and he went straight on the defensive because it was like I was accusing him of something that hadn't even happened. He was mad because I'd ignored all the nice things he'd said and focused on the negative. I couldn't let it go and we went to bed not talking, which made me feel even worse. I told him in the heat of the moment that I was going to get the plane home the next day, and he just answered, 'What time's your flight?', which is quite funny when you look back on it but wasn't at the time! We woke up the next morning and thought, 'What are we doing? Why are we rowing?' So, we kissed and made up.

'What time's your flight?'

THINGS I WOULD ASK JACK NOW IF I HAD ANOTHER CHANCE TO DO THE LIE DETECTOR TEST

- Will you propose when I'm 24?

- What's my ring going to look like?

- When are you going to cook me dinner?

- When are you actually going to book me a nice hot holiday?

I can honestly say that since I've been out of the villa and living with him, I've had no moments whatsoever when I've doubted Jack. I trust him more than anything. I'm too embarrassed to watch that argument back, because I really did overreact and it's cringe to even think about it.

MY BEST LOVE ISLAND MOMENTS

- *OUR FIRST DATE ON THE BEACH* – It was so lovely to spend some time one-on-one. Well, five-on-two, if you count the camera crew in our faces, but we had to ignore them as best we could. He looked so handsome in his white shirt (it still wasn't quite as white as his teeth though) and I fancied him so much. He was saying all this lovely stuff about what he wanted to do when we got out of there, and I thought, 'Maybe he is the one after all?'

· *DAD MEETING JACK ON SKYPE* – I was worried what Dad would think of Jack so it made me so happy that he liked him and approved. 'Babe, he's lovely,' Dad assured me. 'You've found a proper geezer in there.' Then I got Jack in to say hello, and Dad told him, 'I tell ya what I love about ya. I love the fact that you got a little derby [stomach], you've got so much charisma. Listen, it takes a brave man to bowl into that gaff, they're all ab'ed up and ain't got nothing about them. No disrespect yeah. Proper geezer.'

· *JACK TELLING ME HE LOVED ME.*

· *THE FINAL SPEECHES* – We were all dressed up and it was so breathtaking, everyone was really emotional. I've told Jack that if things get tough between us at home I want a recoupling speech. I said to him the other day, 'If you ever do anything that really gets me down or upsets me and I feel like we're at breaking point, I want you to stand up in the living room and I want you to tell me why you wanna couple up with me!' He thinks I'm nuts and it's bizarre but I'm serious. I'm going to text him and say, 'I want a coupling up speech tonight.'

- *OUR LAST DATE IN THE HOT AIR BALLOON.* I looked at Jack up in the sky and felt like, 'We're free and we're doing this together, we're just going nowhere but up', and he had his little white T-shirt on. I really fancied him.

- *MY NAN AND BRUV COMING INTO THE VILLA.* When they walked in I was really choked up; it was so beautiful to see them. We'd been away from our families for weeks so it felt amazing to have a bit of comfort and a cuddle. They looked so cute.

What Would Dani Do?

♡

How long did the dates take to film?

@zoesaunderson

Zoe, 20, Kent

A couple of hours at least. You had to film the slow-mo stuff walking in and then occasionally pick up a couple of shots from different angles but the rest was as it happened.

MY WORST *LOVE ISLAND* MOMENTS

- *FINDING OUT JACK HAD CHEATED ON TWO OF HIS EXES.* He might have protested that it was 'only two' but that made no difference. I didn't want anything to do with him after that and ended up dumping him for a bit.

- *HAYLEY NEARLY COUPLING UP WITH JACK.* After me and Jack split briefly, Hayley wanted to couple up with him because she didn't like Eyal any more. There was a moment when we all sat on the grass and played a game of truth or dare, and someone asked who else we'd rather be with. Hayley said 'Jack' and Jack said 'Hayley'! I was gutted and fuming in equal measure. What an arsey move! He told me afterwards that he just wanted to see my reaction. Well, he got it, didn't he – because I stormed off and then started crying! Looking back, it was just him playing the game as it should be played. It was so early on in the show that we didn't know each other properly. And I hadn't told Jack I still liked him so it was the only way he could find out my feelings.

· *CASA AMOR.* When Jack was with the boys and I knew his ex Ellie was in there, it was without doubt the worst time of my life.

· *THE LIE DETECTOR TEST.* This show really knew how to push people's buttons.

· *SAMIRA LEAVING.* She was one of my best mates in the villa and for her to want to go because she missed Frankie was so sad, even though I understood. The worst part is now that they're not even together so she should have stayed!

· *GEORGIA HAVING TO FACE JOSH RECOUPLING WITH KAZ AFTER CASA AMOR.* She had chosen to stick with him but he pied her. I felt so awful for her. She was fuming and kept saying, 'I was so loyal, Josh' (she said that a lot in the villa though, to be fair). I felt bad because I was happy and she wasn't. Looking back now, it's clear Josh formed a really really strong bond with Kaz – even Georgia will admit that – but it didn't make it any easier for her to swallow.

- *THE FIGHT NIGHT* when everyone was bitching about the Georgia 'kiss or no kiss' with Jack Fowler. That just went on and on and turned ridiculous.

Never in this world did I think we would win. I thought it would be Josh and Kaz because he'd come through so much to be with her. We were together from day one but we were just normal and got on with our day – we didn't give any drama! What was interesting about us two?!

I was so nervous on the final night. Megan and Wes came 4th, then to my shock Josh and Kaz were called out next. After that it was between Laura – who had now coupled up with a lovely guy called Paul – and me and Jack! I loved Laura, she'd been through so much shit in there having been dumped by both Wes and later Jack Fowler. I thought she had a good chance of winning because she was a really sweet girl. She and Paul deserved it just as much as me and Jack.

'And this year's *Love Island* winners are . . . Jack and Dani!'

When Caroline said our names, I was in disbelief.

What the hell?? How had this even happened? I've never won anything in my life, not even a fiver on a scratch card.

I can't even tell you what was going through my mind because it's all such a blur. We hugged each other and held each other tight. We had done it and we were so happy. There was one last big dramatic moment on the show where the winning couple is asked if they will split the £50k, or if one of you will keep it to yourself. But obviously Jack was going to split it. Let's be honest, his life wouldn't have been worth living otherwise! It wasn't about the money anyway, it really wasn't. Having Jack was good enough for me – I felt like I'd won the lottery a trillion times over and I was the luckiest girl in the world.

Jack and I wouldn't be together if we'd met in the outside world, or at least we wouldn't have lasted very long. I know that for a fact. *Love Island* was like two months of couples therapy because you can't run away from your emotions. In the real world, if you have a problem, or fall out, you don't process it or discuss it – you just slam the phone down or go and get pissed with your mates. And that's what's so great about a show like that; it encourages people to share emotions and be open about how they're feeling. It rewards people for being genuine. There's no time for game-players because they're voted off. So, whenever I hear anyone criticising the show, I tell them that it's about honesty and openness.

And surely that's a brilliant lesson to teach young people?

145

WHAT LOVE ISLAND TEACHES YOU
THAT SCHOOL DOESN'T

1. People who are open with their emotions are the winners

2. You should always go with your heart and what makes you happy

3. Talk about how you are feeling – it's the only way to solve things

4. Love makes the world go around

5. You don't need to do anything you don't want to do

6. Be honest because fakeness always gets found out

7. It's about how strong you are as a person, not about how educated you are

Chapter Six

Relationship Rules

Before meeting Jack on *Love Island*, I literally had the worst luck with boys. I hadn't actually had that many relationships, which made the fact that most of them were absolute rubbish even harder to take. It meant that I'd lost all faith in finding someone who would treat me properly.

What Would Dani Do?

I've been dating this guy for a good while and he wants to keep our relationship private but I want to post pictures of us when we are going out and getting dressed up. He doesn't like it; does that mean he's not that into me or am I being silly? It's nice to post pics sometimes!

Lisa

That is weird. On the one hand, you don't have to sit and parade your relationship to the world because it's no one else's business but, equally, if you want to show your boyfriend off then you should be able to. If he doesn't want you posting a picture there might be something dodgy happening. If you want to put up a photo, then post it; it's not like you are doing anything wrong or taking a picture of him looking awful, is it? If he gets the hump about it then you know he's not right. I'm sorry but I'm sure it means there's something going on.

X X X

What Would Dani Do?

♡

Would you still date a guy you really, really like if he had a bad reputation with other girls?

I think it really depends. You can't always judge a boy by his past mistakes. If I did that I would never have been with Jack because I know that before he met me he was a Jack the Lad. Perhaps a boy can change for the right girl. You will never know unless you try. So, give him a go. And if it doesn't go well then at least you know you tried and won't spend time afterwards thinking, 'What if?'

After my first boyfriend, I dated another guy for a few months who managed to make me feel better and pick me up again. But he was more of a mate and even though he was an amazing guy, I couldn't make myself fancy him, so I had to end it. My mum loved him and thought I should have given him more of a chance, but you can't force yourself to want to snog the face off someone, can you?

After that, I went the other way and started seeing someone I really fancied who charmed the pants of everyone he met.

But that was the problem! He was a liar and was seeing loads of other girls behind my back. He didn't even make me his official girlfriend, which meant I didn't feel I had much of a leg to stand on when it came to demanding where he was, so I ended up letting him walk all over me. He wasn't controlling or malicious (and I'd still say hi to him now if I saw him in the street because despite everything I did like him), but he was a major player. And a major headfuck! He would whisk me off for lovely meals and take me on amazing dates and then not contact me again for a few days and go AWOL. It was like I was always the side dish in Nando's. I was just the fried halloumi when all I wanted to be was the full chicken.

I asked my dad for advice on what to do because he knew what made men tick – and he told me, 'He's not for you, babe. He's keeping you like his little secret, which means he doesn't have to go public and can do what he wants.' So once again I was in tears every night asking my friends why it always happened to meeeeeee . . . ?

'I was just the fried halloumi when all I wanted to be was the full chicken'

There's one positive about dating loads of wrong 'uns though. I've learnt the hard way how to spot the danger signs so I know what *not* to put up with!

DANI'S DATING DANGER SIGNS

- HE DOESN'T REPLY TO PHONE CALLS.

- HE TEXTS YOU TO SAY HE WILL COME OVER TO YOURS, BUT THEN DOESN'T TURN UP.

- HE LOOKS IN THE MIRROR MORE THAN YOU DO.

- HE FLIRTS WITH YOUR FRIENDS . . . a bit too much.

- HE KEEPS ASKING QUESTIONS ABOUT YOUR FAMOUS DAD. Before I went on *Love Island* I was asked out by a really fit boy who came into the pub where I worked. I was so excited because my manager let me leave my shift early to go out with him. He took me to a really lovely restaurant, and I couldn't believe how good-looking he was. He was funny too and we were having the best time. Until he beckoned over one of the waitresses, pointed at me and said, 'Guess who her dad is?' I was gutted. He'd only gone out with me because my dad was famous. What a shit.

- HE DOESN'T COMPLIMENT YOU, he just asks why you're dressed in that outfit.

- HE LIES ABOUT WHERE HE IS.

- *HE BUYS YOU CRAPPY PRESENTS* like bath bombs. I hate bath bombs; why do they exist? My nan's mate always buys me bath bombs. Just give me a fiver, I don't need a bath bomb.

- *HE IS A MASTER MANIPULATOR* and always brings up your past mistakes, stuff that doesn't really matter but he pretends it does just to point-score.

- *HE IS WAY TOO POSSESSIVE AND QUESTIONS YOUR EVERY MOVE* – 'Who were you with? Why were you there?!' This type of behaviour is weird and creepy – no boyfriend should be allowed to stop you going out with your friends. And definitely should never demand to know your passwords. In fact, don't share them at all. I've heard of girls who give their Instagram passwords to the guy they are seeing and I think, 'Are you joking!?' They're your passwords for a reason.

- *THEY DEMAND 'SEX TEXTS'.* I hate people who think it's their right to ask for sexy pictures. You don't need to send them. If you want to send them then that's fine, but don't be forced into it and please remember that once you have sent a picture like that it's there forever. So think very, very carefully before you do anything. They could come back to haunt you and then anyone can see them – not just the person you sent it to. Boys have asked me for pictures and I've told them to shove it up their arse. Besides, I did try to take one once and it was a disaster – I took it in the shower because I thought if I looked a bit wet it would detract from the fact I didn't have a clue what I was doing. I tried all these different angles and in the end the whole thing steamed up and I looked like a drowned animal who'd just been caught in a storm and then run over. *There's no way any boy was getting them!*

What Would Dani Do?

♡

I keep getting mugged off by this boy I've been chatting to for 3 months. We've been on a few dates and now he's always cancelling last minute but still texts me.

I think he must like you to be texting you and if he's a busy guy then try be a bit understanding of that. But at the same time, you probably need to confront him about it and be upfront because otherwise you can't move forward. The only way it will be a relationship is if you both spend time together and see each other. Otherwise you will just be mates. So, speak to him and if he's not into it then you know he's a time-waster. And no one likes a time-waster!

MY PERFECT COUPLE

They've definitely had their challenges, but Mum and Dad are the epitome of the perfect couple as far as I'm concerned. They are the yin to each other's yang, the ironed bed sheets to the lump who lies in them, the cupcake to the man who eats it . . .

Mum actually proposed to Dad with a cupcake. He got up one morning and saw it in the kitchen saying 'Will you marry me?' (and then he ate it a few hours later!). They'd always spoken about getting hitched but it had never seemed the right time because us pesty kids kept coming along, also Dad was really busy with work or something else was going on like moving house. I think my dad popped the question about ten years ago but my mum told him he was having a laugh! So, it's typical of my mum that she's the one to ask him. She just decided one day that she wanted to do it.

My mum gets in these moods where she suddenly really, really fancies my dad and gets all soppy with him. She'll ring me up and tell me, 'Oh, your dad is looking really fit today, Dan.' We're more like mates than mum and daughter so it doesn't bother me when she talks about him in that way (although obviously there are limits!).

The wedding was such an emotional day. I was maid of honour. Mum turned into Bridezilla in the run-up, because every single one of her personas wanted to get involved in the organising, but the day itself was just incredible. It was Spanish-themed because of Bruv, and all the little page boys were dressed as cute matadors. My cousins and my sister were bridesmaids too. I loved my dress – it was white and tight-fitted all the way down – while Mum's was just incredible and she looked like a proper Cinderella. The cake theme continued at the reception – everyone was given a cupcake with 'Loved up to fuck' written in icing round the edge! There were fireworks at the end and their song was 'Fire' by Kasabian. My dad didn't have a clue what was going on until he arrived on the day. Mum used to joke, 'This whole thing is going to be a big surprise for you, isn't it, Dan?!'

Dad said he hardly slept the night before. Partly because he was nervous, and also because he was sharing a room with my Grandad Tony who snored the whole night, so Dad ended up chain-smoking in the bathroom.

I had to walk up the aisle in front of Mum and I was petrified because everyone was looking at me. Considering what I now do you probably think it's weird that I don't like being centre of attention! The whole day was so heartfelt and overwhelming and my sister Sunnie wrote a poem for them.

Ironically my mum and dad had their toughest time after the wedding. I'm not sure whether it was fueled by jealousy or what, but suddenly all these girls came out of the woodwork selling stories to the papers, trying to split them up. My mum has always had to put up with the shit that comes with my dad being in the public eye but this time was so much worse. There were stories coming out from his past and no matter how strong the pair of them were it was bound to get to a point where Mum couldn't help but question things. Mum would say to me, 'I've been with this man for so many years and now we're finally married – why is this all happening now?' She still trusted him completely but she was really feeling the pressure of it all. The press got on a roll. One story came out, then someone else jumped on the bandwagon, so it was just one thing after another. In my other ear, Dad was saying it was all a load of rubbish and couldn't understand why she was believing what she was reading. He would say, 'She's moaning but none of those stories are true!' I told him he needed to give her some time before he went to talk to her. Which he did.

These days they're more solid than they've ever been. They've been spending loads more time together and Mum feels like she did when they were 14; they've fallen in love all over again.

Dad knows what Mum likes and is always doing such cute little things to show her he loves her. He'll take her to fancy restaurants like Gordon Ramsey's, or they'll go for a nice sushi (Dad loves his sushi!) and he knows if he gets her an almond croissant and a hot chocolate that's the way to her heart. Sometimes he'll run her a bath and give her a foot massage. She doesn't like to admit she's affectionate but she's a right softie deep down.

In relationships when bad stuff happens it can end up making you both stronger. And you just need to learn what makes each other tick in order to keep things going down the right path.

DANI'S RELATIONSHIP RULES

1. NO GAMES

Stop with all the game playing! I know so many examples of when girls or guys have been in couples and played hard-to-get or have been all 'treat them mean' – then, once they have been dumped, they realise what they've lost and start saying, 'But I love you!' By that point it's too late. Just tell them how you feel from the start and quit all the messing about! Emotions are a good thing; they're what make you bond and bring you closer.

2. DON'T DO ARGUMENTS ON TEXT

If you have the 'ump with each other then it's better to get it out in person than over a text. Don't ask him, 'What's the matter? Please tell me?!' DO NOT BEG. Because he will love it and say, 'Nothing', then carry on being in a mood. Instead, just let him get on with it and say, 'OK, let me know when you're going to be an adult and then we'll have a discussion.' Don't do it over text. It's better to go out and turn your phone off until you get home than do that. Words in print only look worse than when you speak to each other. With texting, you can get angry and bitter and say things you don't mean and then it's there forever as evidence. If you can't meet in person it's far better to do the phone call and have a scream at each other, because it's over and done with and afterwards no one can remember exactly what was said (unless he's recording it all – in which case dump him anyway!). It also really pisses me off with WhatsApp when people have clearly read your message – because the blue ticks are on! – but then they just don't reply! What is that about? Those blue ticks have a lot to answer for. It makes me mad!! You can see people are online but just aren't replying to you. I'm sure 'the blue tick syndrome' is responsible for a few nervous breakdowns.

3. DON'T TAKE THE PISS

Don't take each other for granted or take kindness for a weakness.

4. TRUST EACH OTHER

You need to have honesty and truthfulness in any relationship. Once the trust goes, it's game over, because you're just paranoid all the time and it makes you turn into someone you're not.

5. DON'T DO JEALOUSY

Don't do the jealousy thing, it never works. The only jealousy around should be you making other people jealous that you both have such a great relationship.

6. MAKE SURE YOU TREAT EACH OTHER LIKE BEST MATES

You should be so comfortable that you can completely be yourself around each other and can properly belly laugh over things. You still need your girly mates but your boyfriend is a friend too – that's why he's called your boyfriend.

7. BUT IF YOU STOP FANCYING THEM . . . START TO WORRY

You've got to fancy each other for a relationship to work. You need to have sexual chemistry where you want to grab hold of them! Otherwise you're just in the friend zone.

8. DON'T GIVE THEM EVERYTHING

My mum has always said to me, 'Never give a man one hundred per cent of your love. Ninety per cent is enough.' And I think, no matter what you feel about a guy, she's right. You always need to keep a bit of yourself back for you.

'Never give a man 100% of your love. 90% is enough'

What Would Dani Do?

♡

My ex broke up with me a year ago saying he didn't love me any more. A year on and he's in a new relationship, for 4 months. I think I still love him and I don't know whether to send him a message to let him know or just leave it be. We had such an intense and wonderful 18-month relationship and he's hard to get over! What would Dani do? Message him or move on?

@ejperrett

Ellie, 25, Plymouth

You know what? If he's in a new relationship you have to let him move on. You will find your happiness one day but just let him be, because sometimes you have to accept that things end for a reason. Once you meet someone else you will realise why things didn't work out with him.

ME AND JACK

I definitely put some barriers up when I first met Jack on *Love Island* (and I'm way too embarrassed to watch the episode back where I have a go at him over 'lie-detector-gate'!) but as I said earlier, being holed up in the villa with no way out forced us to be honest about our feelings and open up in a way that we probably wouldn't in the outside world. And after that I trusted him 100%.

Jack is so sweet and he knows how to fill me with confidence. He'll always tell me, 'You look beautiful today', which is something I never had in previous relationships. It's so important to have someone who builds you up like that – it sets you up for the day and is like a confirmation that you're doing alright. I love his family too. The minute I walked into his mum's house after *Love Island,* I felt like I'd come home. It was so cosy; I just wanted to put my pyjamas on straight away (I didn't though, because his nan was coming round and I thought it might be disrespectful!). His mum gave me a cuddle and said, 'Come here, Dan' – she was so warm and inviting.

When Jack met my dad, he was really nervous at first and kept saying, 'I hope he likes me', but I knew they'd click. We got an Indian takeaway and my dad was asking him loads of questions about what made him tick and what he wanted to do. He laughed when Jack said he was going back to selling pens: 'Jack, mate, what the fuck are you talking about? You're famous now, fella!' Dad's really taken him under his wing as I think he sees himself in him a bit. They've become like proper mates and I can leave them alone together now without worrying; it's really cute.

We've both been so busy since *Love Island* that we've had to make an effort to go on 'date nights' and spend proper time together. We tried to avoid telling everyone what we're doing all over social media either too (I have learnt the hard way it can backfire on you!).

1. I can't be bothered with having to update my Instagram all the time.

2. Why have we got to advertise what we are doing? We shouldn't have to tell people we are on a date just to prove that we're still a couple and haven't split up.

3. You miss so many beautiful moments in the world by just putting up Instagram stories on your phone – it's like when people are at concerts and they just film the whole thing. They might as well sit at home and watch it on YouTube! Besides, who sits and watches their Instagram stories back to 'relive the moment'? No one, that's who!

When me and Jack are together we really, really laugh. We adore each other and have exactly the same sense of humour and are quite sarcastic about stuff. We love watching comedy programmes on TV and funny observational stuff. Jack's got a kid's brain sometimes and does stupid things with weird noises and silly walks, which makes me belly laugh.

We were staying at this hotel in Edinburgh at the end of last year, and there was a bowl of sweets on the reception desk. I saw it and said, 'Oh look – fudge!', and we both took one and stuffed it in our mouths as the manager was checking us in. Then we helped ourselves to another, and another and another . . . I don't even remember what the manager looked like, because we were both too busy with our faces in the fudge. Then another guy from the hotel picked up the bowl and gave the whole thing to us! Me and Jack were laughing for ages after that. What greedies!

There's an Italian restaurant underneath the flat we moved into, so we would go down there and have a nice bit of dinner sometimes when we couldn't be bothered to cook. One night, when we first moved in, we went on a bar crawl all along the River Thames, which runs past, and we ended up pissed as farts in All Bar One, befriending this random guy called Patrick, who we proceeded to drag around with us for the rest of the evening. I can't remember much, but I know me and Jack both kept telling him how much we loved him. We woke up the next morning with stinking hangovers but didn't mention Patrick once. We've still not spoken about that night since!

What Would Dani Do?

♡

What's it like living with Jack? Thanks Dani!

@leilapryddx

Leila, 13, Swansea

If I'm honest, it's really hard having a relationship in the limelight. People said Love Island *was the place where couples got tested the most, but for us that part was easy; you're together all the time, you don't have any drunken rows because you're only allowed two drinks a night, you have all your meals prepared for you, you're all over each other and he's not going out with his mates 'til God knows what time in the morning! It's since we've come out into the real world that we've been put to the test.*

We moved into our flat within days of winning the show, but sometimes living together was more of a curse than a blessing! We mainly argued because I didn't think he listened to me and said I was moaning all the time. But as I tried to tell him, if he listened I wouldn't moan! I would say to him, 'Jack, we live in a world where I'm working as much as you are. I can't be your pretty little housewife with a feather duster. I'm tired; we're gonna have to work at this as a team.'

Jack isn't clean at all. He is really REALLY messy. One day, he drank a can of Coke and then left the empty can in the fridge! I saw it, and yelled, 'Why the hell is there an empty can of Coke in here?' (Admittedly I had my period but still!) He looked at me all sheepishly; 'Oh no, Dan, you see, what I've done is, I've basically drunk the can of Coke and then I accidentally put it back in the fridge, but I forgot I'd done it.' What does that even mean and why would you even do that?

I've learnt now that I need to compromise. Jack is just messy. And that's not the big important stuff. If I'm stressed, then Jack really calms me down. Like when we signed up for the flat in the first place I was really flapping because the landlord needed our bank statements and I couldn't find mine. Jack said, 'Dan, it's fine', and he sorted it all out. On the other hand, if he's panicking about something I usually know how to make him feel at ease. And if he's had too much to drink I'll get him home and feed him McDonald's to sober him up! So, we balance each other out in that way.

DANI'S DATING RULES

WHAT TO DO ON A BAD BLIND DATE

If you end up on a date with someone you don't fancy, try not to be too drastic by climbing out of the toilet window. I don't think that's very fair to the date. You can still enjoy yourself and have a bit of fun before you get home and tell them afterwards you didn't think there was a spark: 'I just don't look at you like that, but thanks for giving me a good time.' At least that way you can go to bed knowing you were polite and respectful. Treat them how you would want to be treated. Although, obviously, if your date is really creepy and tries to touch you up, then please just run. Find you nearest taxi service, leave them ASAP and get home safely!

FLIRTING

I've never been good at being all sexy and flirtatious. The only way I can flirt is by bantering with a boy and being sarcastic to make them laugh. Taking the piss out of someone is far easier for me than flicking my hair in their face and trying to look all sexual. As I've said before, I'm not a sexter either. I would never be someone to get my boobs out for a boy and send them naughty pictures. And I'd never say anything suggestive like, 'I can't wait to get home later'; that's not my style. I've never dressed up sexily for a boy – it's pyjamas, fluffy slippers and eye masks all the way.

x x ♡

LAUGHTER

There's nothing attractive about the sort of boys who stand about in clubs posing, trying to look cool with their fancy watches on, just sipping their drinks. I look at them and think, 'What the hell makes you so powerful?' I prefer it when I see a bunch of boys dancing, pissing about and having a laugh with each other. That to me is fun and friendship. Laughter – that's sexy.

SEX

I've never had sex on a first date but I don't judge girls who do. After all, if you give a boy the 'six date rule', they could still take you on all those dates, have a roll around with you and then clear off at the end of it. If the moment feels right, and you're enjoying each other's company, then just go for it. I don't think there should be any rules. It's just about whether you're comfortable and you are happy to do it. But if you feel in your mind that it's not right, then don't. Always trust your gut instincts. When I have sex with someone, I *really* start liking them, which is why I have to know it's going to be worth it — for their sake as well as mine!

LOOKS

I can't say I have a type when it comes to boys, because every guy I've dated looks different. But I do always go for the same sense of humour and charm. I like a guy to have a little glint in his eye.

DANI'S DILEMMAS

Your mate keeps copying your outfits but doesn't say anything to you about it. What do you do?

Make a joke about it: 'I know you like what I'm wearing but I think maybe let's switch things up a little bit. Your outfits are getting a bit predictable and silly now!' And if that doesn't work then just turn up wearing a monster costume and see if she copies that next time!

You fancy the same boy as your friend and he's asked you out — what do you do?

That's a tricky one. If you and your mate like the same boy then I think neither should go for it. Because if you ended up dating him but still knew your mate fancied him that would be weird. You want your mate to think of your boyfriend like their brother, not someone they want to jump into bed with!

> You've been offered the chance to go away for two weeks with the girls – one of their dads is paying for you all because he's loaded. But it's your boyfriend's birthday while you're meant to be away and you had already told him you would treat him. What do you do?

If you made plans with your boyfriend first then you should honour that. If the holiday with the girls had already been booked then you should do the holiday and take him out when you get back. It's about whichever came first.

> You've just noticed your friend has spinach in her teeth and she's just about to open her mouth to speak to a bloke she's fancied for ages – what do you do?

ALWAYS TELL YOUR MATE! Oh my God! Never let her mug herself off like that. Spinach is green; you can't exactly hide it, can you? I would whisper in her ear, 'I need to talk to you quickly', so she came away from him before she had the chance to open her mouth.

Your mate keeps getting really pissed and making a fool of herself when she's out – what do you do?

Pull her up on it. Be honest because that's what friendship is about. She could end up doing or saying something she can't take back so it's your job to help her out. 'You're not really a good drunk. Let's slow ourselves down, shall we?'

XoXo

Chapter Seven

Friendship Goals

I learned from an early age that girls need to look out for other girls. Me and my mum used to sit and watch *A Little Princess* on a Sunday afternoon, and I remember how I loved the fact that the girl in it was so kind to everyone. It's a lovely little film and really taught me that you need to value friendships, and that what you put out there is what you get back. It's so, so important to look out for each other and be a good person.

I'd like to think I'm a fun friend, someone you can have a laugh with. I'm pretty good at giving advice – but that's because I have mates who give it to me, so I've learnt from the best. I will always guide my girls through anything that they are going through, but I will try to be light-hearted rather than full-on serious about it. I don't believe in encouraging your mate to wallow in their self-pity. If someone is sad I'll say, 'Stop your tears, get out of bed, we're going out!' Because I think it's important to make your friend laugh more than to dissect the reason for their misery for hours. Otherwise, if you've both sat there talking about what's wrong with the world, where's the progress? You just end up making your mate feel shitter! My motto is: let's not listen to Adele; let's listen to Dua Lipa!

'I will always guide my girls through anything that they are going through'

What Would Dani Do?

♡

If you are cheekily texting a man you know is wrong for you, should you tell your bessie mate?

@dixieswdn

Dixie, 20, Ireland

I always tell my best mates everything because I know I will need them if it all goes tits up. There's no point hiding things from your friends because otherwise they shouldn't be your mate in the first place! You have enough people in this world who judge you; your family can sometimes judge you, but your mate is there to make you feel better. I will always, always back my friends, I don't care what they've done. That's why you have best friends. Your mate is going to pull you through it. Your best mate is your soulmate.

*

MY THREE AMIGOS

A true friend is always there when you need them and you can tell them anything and trust them 100%.

My best mates are like long-term relationships and I've known most of them since school. There's Kayleigh, who is like a big sister to me. Her mum was a dinner lady and worked with my nan, and I used to idolise her. She's three years older than me and so she really looked out for me at school. Kayleigh's little like me – just 5' 1" – and I remember she used to have the most brilliant collection of Primark vests; she had them in loads of different colours with frills on. I'd go over to hers for a sleepover and she'd let me wear them. It felt really cool having a mate who was older than me. She was the one who supported me through my first big break-up and that's when I really knew just how special she was. She will get me through anything and everything and she's the first person I will turn to in a crisis. She gives me brilliant advice without telling me what to do.

'A true friend is always there when you need them and you can tell them anything and trust them 100%'

Then there's Charlotte. She always seems to be going through the same shit as me at exactly the same time – whether that's dating rubbish men or just having a hard time with work. We've gone through everything together, and can often be found sitting at the kitchen table at 1 a.m. drinking Malibu out of the bottle and pouring our hearts out. When everything was going wrong the year before I went into *Love Island*, we were drinking and partying loads and would sing our hearts out to Dua Lipa and Zara Larsson. Now she's got a serious boyfriend like me, which is great because it means we can hang out on double dinner dates instead.

Ellie is great for guidance. We have been mates for years but we're so different. Her life has been planned out since she was about 14 when she got the boyfriend she's still with today. She always has a great job and never seems to make mistakes. She's very steady and that's what I love about her.

HOW TO BE A REALLY GOOD MATE

- No pity parties

- FUN FUN FUN

- Listen to them

- Spend time with them

- Pick them up when they are feeling down

- Also praise them when they are doing well

- Always be on the other end of the phone so you are there if ever your mate is in a sticky situation

- Don't become a green-eyed monster

- Have drunken nights (always mop up their sick)

- Trust each other

- Give as much as you get

- Your friends are the family you can choose – so choose wisely!

I know within ten minutes if I'm going to be someone's friend or not. I don't like girls who look down their noses at you but then suddenly get all pally when they've had a drink. Me and my mates always say these girls are not 'one of us' – you should be open and warm from the start and never look other girls up and down. It's just like having a type when it comes to boyfriends – you have that with girls too!

My two biggest no-nos when it comes to other girls are jealousy and lying.

1. I hate jealousy. I just don't get that emotion full stop. I think it's a really ugly trait. I've never been a jealous person. If one of my mates got something lovely, like a pair of Valentinos or a new car, I might say, 'Oh my God, I'm so jealous', but it would be just a turn of phrase. I would mean it in a nice way, as in 'I'm so happy for you'. Jealous friends are the sort who will look down their noses, or dismiss what you have to say, when you tell them a piece of good news. A friendship has to be a two-way thing; even if you have completely different lifestyles, you should be interested in what each other is

doing and what you have to say. I really don't like jealous people at all. I don't get why you'd want to be jealous of someone – you should be pleased for their success! If I notice girls around me acting bitter or jealous, I'll cut them off. I can't be bothered with all that.

2. My mum and dad have taught me that lying is one of the worst traits you can have. They will stick by me no matter what I've done, as long as I'm honest with them. When people lie, it becomes a problem. My mum says she would rather I was a thief than a liar and I feel like that with mates. You have to be able to trust them above everything else.

MY *LOVE ISLAND* LADIES

Although *Love Island* was about being in a couple, I always knew I wouldn't survive in there without forming some proper friendships with the girls. On the one hand, you're meant to be concentrating on which boy you want to be with, but you definitely need your girls as well. It was tough in that villa at times, so without having mates to confide in we'd have all gone nuts. I didn't make best friends with everyone, but there are some ladies who will always be close to my heart.

GEORGIA

Although she came in slightly later than me, Georgia was one of the girls I got on with best. I love her honesty and just how straight up she is. Don't get me wrong, she did drive me mad at times because we're very different – she'd run around doing cartwheels or jumping in the pool and wanting to stay up till 5 a.m., whereas I wanted to be in bed by 10 p.m. with my eye mask on. But I could chat to her for hours and we really opened up and supported each other, especially when the boys were in Casa Amor. She gave me a cuddle when I needed a cuddle and I did the same with her; there was no agenda and nothing was done for the cameras and she'll definitely be a friend for life.

SAMIRA

I really love that girl. She's so funny and sassy and has such a sexy walk. We could tell what each other was thinking just from a simple look (like when Jack's ex Ellie walked into the villa and we raised our eyebrows at each other!). In the villa, I would sit and giggle all evening with Samira – she would always build me up if I felt low. She would turn to me and say, 'Look at who you are! You're Dani Dyer – act like her!' And I'd snap right out of my mood.

LAURA

Scottish Laura is just really cute. We were in the show together right from the beginning, so she's extra special to me because we shared the same journey. She needed a lot of comforting because of the shit she had to put up with in the villa, with boys messing her about, so I always tried to be there for her. We text each other a lot now about how we're both feeling; she's found being in the limelight hard at times and I have too so we have a lot in common. And we trust each other implicitly. I know she would never go behind my back on anything.

KAZIMIR

It was tough for Kaz coming into the villa with Josh after Casa Amor, because everyone was so close to Georgia. But I think her and Josh were just lovely together and made a really beautiful couple so it was the right move. She was really kind to me so I haven't got a bad word to say about her. Plus, she always did my eyeliner, which saved me from looking like shit in the evenings!

ALEXANDRA

Although Alex was a really late arrival to *Love Island*, I bonded with her instantly. I only wish she'd been there from the beginning. She has a really nice way about her; she's warm with a good heart and is naturally really funny. There was one moment when she told the girls about the moment when she put her hand down Alex's pants and the way she said it made me absolutely wet myself laughing. She's like a goddess and really sexy but a real girl's girl.

MEGAN

I didn't like what Megan did to Laura by swooping in and taking Wes from her. I thought that was a really muggy thing to do at the time. But her and Wes went on to have a long-term relationship so I know it was worth it in the end. Megan might not be the sort of person I'd usually hang out with but I do really like her. I think she just didn't know how to behave around other girls because she'd not had any proper female friendships before. When a girl says they've never really have girl mates, it usually sends off a load of warning signals and I think, 'Why?' But I don't think it was Megan's fault. I like Megan; she's a very sweet girl. We will never be best friends but she's been through a lot and deserves happiness.

GIRL CODE - THE RULES

1. You have to think about other girls and treat them with respect even if you don't know them very well.

2. You don't ever belittle another girl, you make her feel good. You should always big another girl up.

3. Don't ever get with your mates' boyfriends.

4. Don't go behind another girl's back.

5. Think of that other girl as if it was you – put yourself in her shoes.

What Would Dani Do?

♡

My friend's boyfriend cheated on her with her best friend. I tried to tell her but she doesn't believe me. What should I do?

@itsmayaaa22

Maya, 20, London

Firstly, that's a disgusting thing for him to do, but secondly, it's a difficult one for you. There's only so much you can do really because on the one hand you would want to say to your mate, 'Why would I ever want to lie to you?', but you can only say so much. I think deep down she probably does believe you but doesn't want to admit it. If my best mate turned around to me and said Jack had been cheating on me, my reaction would be, 'No, he hasn't!', but I would be questioning everything in my head. And the truth always does come out in the end and that's when you have to be there for her. But you shouldn't take it upon yourself to go all detective about it and start producing facts and evidence because that's just rubbing it in. You just have to say, 'You might not believe me now, but when the truth does come out I'm here for you.'

What Would Dani Do?

♡

My motivational levels in the morning are so bad! How do you motivate yourself to get up and get on?

@emilycreigh_

Emily, 14, Maidstone

I used to hate mornings but I'm getting so much better. Now I just get up. Don't snooze your alarm, it only makes you feel worse. Just get on with it and get in the shower!

What Would Dani Do?

♡

How do u fix arguments with best friends?

@serenity_sanders_

Serenity, 13, Suffolk

If you're mates and you have a row you usually have each other's best interests at heart even if it doesn't feel like it at the time. You just have to talk to each other and

183

thrash it out. The less arguments the better really. You have enough of those with other people so don't do it with your friends if you can help it.

What Would Dani Do?

♡

What is your favourite meal?

@sineadbarrett14

Sinead, Northamptonshire

I love a Chinese takeaway with my mates. I'm really boring and like special fried rice and curry sauce.

NIGHTS IN V NIGHTS OUT

No hesitation – nights in! I love staying in with my mates, getting a takeaway, a few glasses of wine and putting the world to rights. I feel like night-time is where the Devil's lurking. Nothing good ever happens past midnight. People get drunk and say shit they don't mean. Take it from me – you're better off staying at home!

FRIENDS V FELLAS

I've always been a strong advocate of 'sisters before misters' but I do think it depends on the situation. If me and my best mate fancied the same boy then I would always say it's not worth falling out over. Friendships come first. But now I'm in a relationship with Jack I see him as my friend too and sometimes he will need to take priority. Obviously if one of my mates rang me in bits and needed me to go round, I'd be there in a flash but I wouldn't sack off a date night with Jack to go out with the girls.

TEXTING V TALKING

I can't be bothered with all these different WhatsApp groups. I think they can be really bitchy. For example, why is there a WhatsApp group with seven girls in and then another one with just four of them? What's wrong with those extra three people? Why can't they all be in the same one unless the group of four is just slagging the rest of them off?

Aside from that, I get mixed up and confused with too many different groups on my phone. I have a family one and that's enough. I couldn't keep up with the *Love Island* one either – it did my head in. Everyone was on it so it was impossible to keep up! Also, I didn't really want to be in a WhatsApp group with my boyfriend's ex. And I feel like if we need to talk to each other let's just have an old-fashioned one-on-one conversation, shall we? I don't need to know what you're having for dinner or that you're now getting in the bath. Don't send me essays about it on the phone. NO. I just can't be bothered. My mates don't bother texting me because I hardly ever reply!

THINGS THAT ALWAYS MAKE ME LEAVE
A WHATSAPP GROUP

- Spoiling the ending of a TV show I haven't watched yet.

- Writing loads of separate words instead of a proper paragraph! 'Alright?' . . . 'You good?' Are you thinking before you're writing?!

- When you go to the loo and there are about 180 unread messages waiting for you. I just have to mute those groups (and the good thing is there's an option to mute for a whole year!).

- Once you have muted the group – someone saying, 'Why haven't you said anything? Are you OK?'

- Continuous updates of what someone is doing or what emoticon they are feeling.

- When someone says, 'What you wearing?', I think, 'Here it comes', and then there are about twenty pictures!

- When people add you to groups you didn't ask to be added to and you then get bombarded with annoying updates!

What Would Dani Do?

♡

What's the most important quality to you in a person?

@harybo3

Harriet, 32, St Albans

Kindness. Hands down.

DIFFERENT TYPES OF FRIENDS YOU NEED IN YOUR LIFE

· The fun friend – you always need that person you can ring up and say, 'Babe, I need to go out and enjoy myself.' There's no agenda; you just go out and have a really good time.

· The crazy friend who puts her foot in it and is a bit ditzy – they always make you laugh.

· The stylish friend – everyone has a mate who's got real class and style and is so cool in everything she wears. Someone you can look up to and can lend you her clothes!

· The wise friend – someone to guide you in the right direction and gives you criticism that you might not want but you need. For me now it's also important to have a wise friend who's known me forever and who keeps my feet on the ground.

· The older friend – like an auntie. Someone who has lived life and knows exactly what you're going through. She will say, 'I bet you want to do this and are feeling like this . . .' and they can assure you that things will get better.

· Your best mate – someone you can tell everything to and pour your heart and soul out to. They're more like your sister and your soulmate.

Chapter Eight

Believe In Your Body

What Would Dani Do?

♡

How can I be less self-conscious and more confident. I would be so happy if you answered this because I feel like this all the time.

@janiforlife_xx

Chloe, 15, Carlisle

How would you stop comparing yourself and your body to everyone around you? A daily struggle for myself!

@veritypitts

Verity, 19, Brighton

I know it's really hard but the first thing you need to do is to try to not compare yourself to other people. You might not think it, but I bet everyone you're thinking is better than you is thinking that way about other people themselves. Everyone has their own insecurities deep down – some just don't show them on the outside. The best thing you can do is to think about how you can make your mind feel good, as it's all about what's on the inside that dictates how you feel you look on the outside. My mum has always called it a 'glow' and that's not something physical; it's something in your head. So you need to spend time doing things you enjoy, things that make you happy and be with people who make you laugh and smile. Try and exercise and get outside and look around you – fresh air works wonders for the brain and your headspace!

Whenever you look in the mirror and think something negative, try and push that thought away and instead look at something positive – something you like about yourself (and if you can't think of anything ask your mum or your best mate as they will have loads!). It might sound odd but if you tell yourself positive things every day you can actually train your brain to believe it.

One of the reasons successful athletes win races is because they visualise themselves getting a medal so much that it actually becomes reality. And you can do that when you think about yourself. Spend ten minutes every morning talking to yourself and reminding yourself of all the good things about you. And all the things you think you don't like are probably the stuff that makes you unique and different and special. So think of them as unique rather than bad. It will feel a bit of a chore and like homework, but stick at it and you will be surprised how good you feel once you have done it every day for a few weeks.

Also be nice and kind to other people – it makes you feel nice. The world is magical if you think about it – I mean, how are we even alive?! So, spend time with others who make you feel good and happy and do things that get you out learning new things and keeping occupied.

I'd be lying if I said I never had days where I feel yuk and don't want to leave the house. Yet, instead of wishing I had bigger boobs (I have none!), or a different shaped arse (it's massive – comes from my dad's side of the family!), I have learnt to like and accept what Mother Nature has given me. I'm not one of those people who think they look the bollocks but I do occasionally have a moment in the mirror where I think, 'You look alright today, girl!' I've learnt that the most important part about how you look is how you feel and, therefore, act. As I walked into the villa in *Love Island*, I knew

I wouldn't be the slimmest, prettiest or sexiest girl but I also knew that if I was myself and had fun then hopefully I would make people laugh. And that's one of the most attractive qualities a person can have. I am never going to be a sex icon. I can't do any of those sexy poses like Megan or Laura could. The cameramen on *Love Island* managed to teach me how to flick my hair and do a bit of a flirty walk — we had to do those when we were going on dates and they would edit it all slow motion — but I'm not a sexy person, and I'm cool with that.

SEXY BUSINESS

I didn't really get a lot of attention from boys when I was younger; I wasn't pretty at all and I didn't even need a bra for a long time, which was something they were all obsessed with. I didn't care though. I preferred being mates with boys first and making them laugh. And in the end, that's what got me a few snogs! Most importantly, I was never sexually active at a young age and that's something I'm proud of still. I never offered a boy anything on a plate and never will. I think that's partly down to my Nanny Carol — she's only ever slept with one boy (and that's Bruv). Obviously, I'm not as much of a good girl as she is, but she did teach me to respect myself. She would always say, 'Don't be one of those girls who gives yourself to just anyone, because you don't want a boy to walk down the street and say, "I've had her . . . my mates have had her . . . my cousin has had her".' Don't get me wrong, I've still slept with some boys I wish I hadn't, but I've made sure I'm not the sort of person that boys speak about in that way. Plus, as I've said earlier, I'm a hopeless romantic, so if I sleep with a boy I will want to marry him and that's not something I want to mess my head about with for no reason!

When it came to 'sex talk', it was my dad's mum, Nanny Christine, who would be my go-to. Apparently, I was really, really intrigued about sex education. I would demand to know about it over the dinner table. 'Why do people have sex, Nan?' (She didn't tell me until I was older that it was something people did for fun!). Nanny Christine is a trained counsellor so she's great at listening to people's problems. I have confided in her about bad boyfriends and every type of relationship dilemma and she will always tell me what I needed to hear without sugarcoating things. She would say things like, 'He's manipulating you . . . he's not great for you.' She's a wise one, my Nanny Christine.

NAKEDNESS

I'm quite embarrassed and a bit of a prude when it comes to getting naked in front of people and I've never got dressed up in sexy underwear for a boy. I'm simply not that confident when it comes to things like that. So, you might be surprised to hear that when Jack and I had sex for the first time it was actually *me* putting it on *him* rather than the other way around! I turned to him and grinned. 'So, are we gonna have some fun?' He looked at me and said, 'But we've got to be up in two hours!' Er, was he kidding me?! 'Yes, Jack, I know. TWO HOURS!' I think he'd got so used to us not doing anything in the villa that he didn't think it was ever going to happen. Looking back, it's a good job we were both a bit pissed because it's a lot of pressure having to perform after all that time! I kept thinking, 'This could either be great or this could be really bad!' I hadn't even seen his willy so I was going in blind! I was also a bit worried because he's a couple of years older than me, and I knew he had slept with quite a few women, so I didn't know how I would compare. What if I was rubbish in bed?! Thank God neither of us were disappointed! It's just got better as we've got to know each other more and Jack has always made me feel really body confident. He says he loves my little boobs and would hate it if I ever had a boob job; he likes me looking natural and real. He will always tell me I look beautiful even when I just think I look ordinary. He really keeps me going in that way, which makes me feel lovely.

'It's just got better as we've got to know each other more'

It's not just girls who get worried about their looks. Jack is conscious about his body too but I don't think he opens up enough or admits it to me. He isn't all cut and chiseled like some blokes, which personally I love about him. He says he's cool with his body but then sometimes he will get down if he hears a negative remark. Like one time, he went to the dry-cleaner's and the man there told him he looked like he'd put on weight. Why do people think they have the right to stay that sort of stuff? It's not the same as saying you need a haircut! I know it affected him because he kept talking about it afterwards and I was really mad. I thought, 'Bastards, how dare they say that to you?' I don't get that. People have been horrible to him on social media too and I think it's disgusting to tell someone they have put on weight when they haven't asked your opinion. He now keeps talking about how he wants to get fit again – he used to do boxing, which kept the weight off.

The problem is, I don't think he can because he loves his food so much! He should really look like a balloon, the amount he eats. He doesn't even eat, he just swallows things whole! He told me his mum used to hide food from him and I totally get why. I will buy a bag of crisps and he's inhaled them before I've even put them in the cupboard. But I love the way Jack is; I don't want him to change. I do think he's a bit deluded though – the other day we had to rush to Zara to get him some trousers for an important meeting (he'd turned up to my agent's office in a tracksuit and they told him he needed something smarter as he was seeing a big TV commissioner). When we got there, he picked out a pair of blue chinos and announced, 'I'm going to get a size 32 because I'm on a diet,' and I laughed, 'Er, but you haven't lost the weight yet, Jack. You need to put these trousers on in about two minutes not two months' time!'

SMILE PLEASE!

One of the things I was self-conscious about growing up were my teeth. Four of them stuck out funny and one specific one poked out from the side really weirdly and people would comment on it. So, when I joined the dental practice when

I was 16 years old I got a brace. It hurt like hell and was painful and smelt gross. But it was worth it because I'm quite partial to my gnashers nowadays.

Even though I thought Jack's teeth were VERY bright when I first met him, I'm not so blinded by the whiteness any more. I don't really know why he got them done but he tells me it was because one of them was damaged and he didn't like having to wear a false tooth. Jack's one of those people who will always go to the extreme and doesn't think before he does something. So, he went to a dentist in Turkey because it was cheaper and the process of getting his veneers was meant to take two weeks but he made them do it all in three days.

BODY CONSCIOUS

It's scary to think how young people are when they become aware of their bodies these days. I remember eating chocolate, and crisp sandwiches (cheese and onion ones – yum), and not caring about whether it would give me a big tummy. But now with social media it's so much worse for people. I worry about my sister Sunnie – she's only 11 and already thinks she's overweight. I have to keep an eye on her to make sure she's looking after herself because sometimes she will show me a picture from Instagram and she's scribbled her face out because she doesn't think she looks very nice. She's beautiful! Please remember this whenever you are looking at Instagram – nothing is real, everyone has retouched something about themselves and it's all fake! So don't ever compare yourself and don't spend too long on there either. Your real life is much more important than this pretend world where everyone looks like they have no facial features because they have Facetuned themselves so much!

I danced a lot when I was at primary school so even though I don't have a naturally skinny frame the weight kept off. It wasn't until I was about 14 that I became conscious of my figure. Everyone at school would be counting calories and boasting about skipping lunch so it was hard not to be caught up in it all. Peer pressure can be a dangerous thing and you become obsessed with being skinnier than your friends. Thank God I've never starved myself or made myself sick. I know it happens to some people and that sometimes life seems to get too much and the thought of controlling your body with food feels like the only option – but it's not. Eating disorders are serious issues and can kill. If you are suffering, or know anyone else who is, then the best thing you can do is talk to someone and discuss it, because there are other ways to make yourself feel better.

Thankfully I've not had to deal with it as none of my friends have had eating problems either – we love our Chinese takeaways too much! I think I have a healthy relationship with food because I know I need to watch what I eat so I just never overindulge. I will be good in the week and exercise and then I will treat myself to a takeaway or something I fancy on a weekend. Life is hard enough so you should make time to enjoy it — and food is a big part of life for me.

FIT FADS

I've been on some right odd diets in my time. There was something called The Clean 9 diet, which everyone was doing a few years ago. You have nine days of drinking disgusting aloe vera shots and basically living on aubergines and tomatoes! I could only stomach seven days because the whole thing made me feel so faint and ill. I had zero energy and couldn't go to the gym and that's what I enjoy most. My trainer David told me to come right off it because it was dangerous.

You might think I'm crazy but I love how exercise makes me feel. When I'm not busy I like to go to the gym four to five times a week and I love running too — it helps me clear my head. I love feeling sweaty and like I've worked hard enough to earn a few slices of pizza. They say you get good endorphins from exercise and for me that's a really addictive feeling. Dad does yoga and meditation to relax but I like

At the screening of my first proper film — look how proud my dad is! Such a softie.

Out in South Africa filming my short-lived first TV appearance, *Survival of the Fittest.*

First day on Love Island, waiting to be picked. God, I was nervous!

Me and Jack's first date, getting to know each other and talking about the future.

When Jack asked me to be his girlfriend – I was so happy – I'll never forget this moment.

Giving it straight to Georgia. She did my head in sometimes, but I loved our girly chats and we were always there for each other.

The final of *Love Island* – miss these guys so much!

What a dilemma! Luckily he made the right choice!

Such a proud moment, still pinching myself now.

At the launch of my clothing line with my biggest supporters!

So lovely to have my girls at the launch wearing my range – best mates are always there for you!

Raising a drink with Adam from In The Style to our success.

My own bus! Not many people can say that, eh?

Out in the real world with this (loyal!) babe.

Feeling loved up in Rome with my handsome boy.

Nothing beats a glass of wine with an amazing girl friend.

In Majorca with Bruv and Nan – where their love story began.

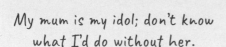

My mum is my idol; don't know what I'd do without her.

It meant the world to me to end an incredible year by performing alongside my dad in *Nativity*. Would do it again in a heartbeat!

Beginning the 8-day Mount Kilimanjaro climb for Comic Relief with an incredible bunch of people. I am nervous, but I feel so honoured to have been given this opportunity to make a difference.

feeling the aches and pains afterwards. Plus, I can't handle the idea of being in yoga next to someone's smelly arse; people always let a fart out when they're that relaxed and I don't need to be near that.

EASY EXERCISES YOU CAN DO AT HOME

I do a circuit of three different exercises that I repeat three times, with each time getting less and less so it never feels as much and becomes a bit more manageable.

1. 20 burpees

2. 20 lunges on each leg

3. 50 star jumps

PAUSE

1. 15 burpees

2. 15 lunges on each leg

3. 30 star jumps

PAUSE

1. 10 burpees

2. 10 lunges on each leg

3. 15 star jumps

END!

My mum is really into colonics, which is a treatment that's meant to be good for detoxifying your body; it cleanses you and gets rid of your toxins. If you don't know what it is . . . you get a tube put up your bum and watch all your poo from years ago get syphoned out! Mum swears by them and says they made her feel great afterwards. It's gross! It's a weird sensation; I didn't enjoy it at all! I felt violated. I walked out the room and I was shaken; I couldn't talk to anyone. I think Mum must be getting commission on them because she sends everyone there – even my dad (he didn't like it either).

No part of my body is sacred with my mum. She even insists on waxing my Nunnie for me. She seems to think she can do it better than anyone else. I went back home the other night for some tea and she ended up making me get on all fours while she did it in the lounge. It really hurt! I was having to take sips of wine to numb the pain while my poor sister Sunnie was trying to watch TV!

TROLLS (SHOULD BE KEPT IN THEIR HOLES!)

No matter how confident you feel or how much you tell yourself not to listen to other people, it's virtually impossible not to be affected by someone criticising you on social media. I can imagine how hard it is for young girls at school to have to put up with people they don't know making judgement on how they look or their weight, because I got trolled myself back in September 2018, the day I launched my clothing collection for In The Style.

I was so chuffed to have been offered the chance to have my own clothing line that this was a massive deal for me. When I arrived at the In The Style offices in Manchester, I was greeted by a massive billboard covered with my face, the whole place was decorated with my name and it made me feel incredible. Jack had come up to support me and we had our photo taken in front of the billboard, which he put it up on his Instagram to say how proud he was. Admittedly, it wasn't the most flattering picture of me – I'm staring up at him and laughing and it's a little bit cringe – but I didn't think anything of it . . . until the comments starting coming.

'Is she pregnant?'

'She looks really bloated.'

'Too many pies.'

'She's let herself go since *Love Island* . . .'

'She's no fashion designer . . . what's she bothering for?'

There was one girl who started it, and then others began joining in. Even though there were loads of nice comments from people telling me they were excited about my clothing launch, it was the negative ones I focused on. Some nice girls tried to stick up for me and said, 'What are you lot talking about???' and 'I don't know why everyone is attacking another girl', but I still felt so upset. It really made me feel deflated and it ruined my whole day. They were such nasty things to say. I thought, 'There are so many things going on in the world . . . why are we making girls feel shit?! Be a girl's girl!!' I don't understand how people can comment on what someone else looks like? It really annoys me that we're in an age where people say we should promote plus sizes and visibility of all shapes, yet you can still get bombarded by nasty comments like that. The ironic thing is that it's these sorts of people who would cry their eyes out if someone said the same to them. They just hide behind their keyboards, messaging abuse. These people are probabably just very insecure.

It infuriates me that I allowed them to make me feel bad. And I hate to admit it, but I started looking at myself differently that day. No matter how much I tried not to worry about it, it still hurt. It was the first time I'd had to deal with such maliciousness from the public. I can understand why some celebrities end up getting surgery if they get attacked like that. And then the public turns on them and says, 'Why the hell have they had work done?' Well, why do you think?

My mum was the first person I turned to. I went to a room and called her, sobbing down the phone. She's been there a thousand times before and is used to getting abuse because she's with my dad. Women are obsessed with him, so Mum has had to put up with a lot. She has learnt to bat most of it away and not let it touch her. She has an in-built confidence about her and she takes no shit. She proper rates herself and will look in the mirror and say, 'I am the nuts', and she is. She doesn't do it in an arrogant way; she's just very self-assured, which I admire about her. She jokes that it's because she has no time to wait for other people to give her compliments so she has to give them to herself.

After I told her what had happened, she said, 'Listen, I've been called every name under the sun but do you think I care? No. I look at myself and I think, "I'm a fucking sort. I've got this", and that's what you need to think, Dani. You are beautiful, you don't look remotely pregnant and you need to remember you are better than the lot of them put together.' She told me to take it in my stride and ignore it. 'Look at all the amazing comments you got, Dani – and you're ruining your big day by listening to the few bad ones?'

'I'm a fucking sort. I've got this'

I didn't write anything back to the comments that day. I knew it wouldn't be a good idea. If I hadn't been famous I'd probably have got angry and written something like, 'Who do you think you're messaging?' But I knew I couldn't show the demon side of Dani. She only comes out when she has to stick up for herself and no one needs to see her! I put out a statement the next day instead.

I was in the car on the way to film for *Celebrity Juice* and I thought, 'Fuck it, I need to have my say.' I wrote back to one of the haters:

I'm actually so hurt and disgusted about people's comments! It's so so rude. It's all about supporting each other. As a girl, you're meant to bring someone up, mate, and make them feel good! Or if you think I look like shit, text your mate it, don't publicise it! Don't comment horrible things, it's nasty and it will get you NOWHERE in life! Every angle is different and I'm sure as a girl you would know that. In other pictures from that day, my stomach doesn't look like that. So really have a long hard think on what you say before you do it, because we live in a world where every girl is beautiful, no matter what angle or shape. Just think!

What Would Dani Do?

♡

How do I handle the trolls and bullying on social media?

@suzie_barton
Suzie, Crowthorne

· *Ignore the negative comments – block them, delete them!*

· *Focus on people who say nice things and read them over and over*

· *Remember you will have some pictures that don't look so flattering but that's life! Most people do not look like they do in their Instagram pictures. Social media is fake*

· *If it gets you down, delete the app for a bit and walk away – too much phone time is bad for your brain. Go and look at the trees (seriously, they are pretty!) and talk to people you love and who make you laugh, go and watch your favourite film, book a weekend away doing something fun with your friend – IN REAL LIFE!*

What Would Dani Do?

♡

Do you feel pressure to change yourself, fillers etc? You're gorgeous as you are but we all compare ourselves x

@sarahpartridge1
Sarah, 29, West Midlands

I'm putting it out there: I've never liked my nose. It's big and comes around the corner way before I do. Ever since that boy at school called me 'Carrot Nose' when I was 12, I've wanted to have a nose job but I couldn't afford it. But I feel like I can't get one done now I've been on Love Island! I'm too scared to do something like that to myself because I don't want to let anyone down, or make it seem acceptable to change the way you look. I don't want to upset the girls who follow me and support me. I want girls to feel beautiful in their bodies and that they haven't got to change the way they look to feel good. I feel like I would be betraying that if I changed something about myself.

SURGERY

(My dad keeps saying he wants surgery on his man boobs. He reckons he's developed a C-cup bra size and they really bother him. It makes me laugh that he hates them so much. He talks about them all the time and calls them his 'Lills'.)

I got lip fillers done a year ago just because I wanted them but I hated how it made me look. My lips have settled down now but some of the filler has stayed so it still looks like I've got something in. When they were first done, my nan said I looked like a duck and my mum said I looked like I'd been walloped in the mouth. It's not worth it either because the pain is excruciating!

Although all the girls were gorgeous in *Love Island*, I never once looked at one of them and wished I had their body instead. No matter what shape we were, we all had days where we'd be self-conscious and worried about how we looked. As my mum always says, confidence comes from within and that's what makes someone shine (the same goes for people who look good on the outside but are ugly on the inside – their attractiveness soon disappears as soon as they show their true personality). Even if you're the most stunning creature on the planet, if you're having a bad day you will feel like you look terrible. Megan has one of the best bodies I've ever seen, but the silly thing is she's probably the most insecure of the lot of us. Ultimately, I have learned to make the best of my body. I have muscly legs and I'm quite short so I wear wedges to make myself feel longer. I have accepted my nose is part of me and that's what gives me character. I have a shapely bum so I make sure I wear things that show it off rather than trying to hide it. And I've discovered that the left side of my face is far better than the right – so I make sure I stand that way in pictures (so if you see me on Instagram constantly looking in the same direction now you know why!).

'Even if you're the most stunning creature on the planet, if you're having a bad day you will feel like you look terrible'

Chapter Nine

Dress Your Best

I've never had a proper 'style icon' who I stalked obsessively on Instagram, but I used to love the outfits Effy from E4's *Skins* wore – all oversized jumpers, leather jackets and baggy T-shirts. I think the actress who played her, Kaya Scodelario, is amazing. She's so talented and inspirational. I actually might be a little bit in love with her. I have always liked my mum's style too – she's quirky and wears caps and baggy tracksuit pants, Dr Martens with jeans or little fur gilets (which I pinch out of her wardrobe). And my dad has good dress sense – he knows what works for him and usually wears jeans, T-shirts and leather jackets. He bought me my very first leather jacket from his favourite shop, All Saints, and I've never looked back. They're really expensive, but the leather is so soft you could sleep in it. There was a time when I'd always think you had to really tart yourself up so I'd wear little black dresses with heels and dodgy fake tan, but as I've got older I've worked out what suits me best. I prefer mixing stuff up a bit – like pairing trainers with a cute, pretty playsuit, or a smart shirt with jeans, or a little co-ord denim jacket and skirt with pumps.

My motto is that you should always dress for yourself. I want to be comfortable but trendy at the same time. I'm not a boobs out, bum out kind of girl. I'm more conservative in how I style things because I think you don't need your boobs or bum showing to look sexy. I'm quite girly and commercial in my style, which I guess is relatable to most people because I'm not too out there or over the top with my love of designer pieces.

MY STYLE RULES

- *REMEMBER THERE ARE NO RULES!* If you are wearing something and you feel great, then that will come across in your whole look, but if the clothes are wearing you then you won't look your best.

- *DRESS TO SUIT YOUR SHAPE*, not to suit the fashion. Wear whatever you feel comfortable in. Someone can tell you what to wear a thousand times, but it doesn't mean you will feel good in it. My stylist Ellis said to me recently, 'There is nothing sexier than a girl who embraces her shape and is comfortable in her own body' – and she's right!

- *DRESS FOR YOU* – not for any man!

- *LOVE WHAT YOU'RE WEARING*, don't just like it.

- *DON'T DRESS UP EVERY SINGLE DAY.* It won't make you feel special when you go out otherwise. You know when you're wearing something you feel good in because you have a bit of a sass.

- *ACCEPT* the fact that when you get something new it will never feel as good as the first time you wear it!

- *TRAINERS* go well with pretty dresses – change things up a bit.

- *IF YOU'VE GOT SHORT LEGS* and are about to have your picture taken, wear wedges!

- *DON'T COPY WHAT YOUR MATE WEARS* if she has boobs and you don't.

- *BE REAL* – if I'm going for dinner I will often wear a floaty dress so I don't have to worry about feeling bloated!

- *SPEND TIME LOOKING FOR THE RIGHT PAIR OF JEANS* – they are a crucial part of the wardrobe and the decision can't be rushed!

- *DON'T BE SCARED OF COLOUR.*

- *DON'T BUY SHOES YOU CAN'T WALK IN* – never a good look.

- *FIND YOUR OWN STYLE AND STICK TO IT* – this makes shopping so much easier and more fun.

DRESS TO IMPRESS

I love my clothes but I've definitely never thought of *myself* as a style icon! So, when I had two different brands fighting to sign me up for my own clothing range I nearly ate my shoes in shock.

My agent, Adam, arranged for me to meet both clothing brands on the same day. Which was great except for the fact that it was the morning after the *Love Island* wrap party, and I was so hungover I looked like I needed an entire body transplant. The two meetings couldn't have gone more differently. The first one felt really cold and impersonal – the people from the brand showed me a PowerPoint presentation that looked like it was the same thing they wheeled out for every celebrity and they told me they would sign me for six months. I know I should have been flattered but I just didn't get a good vibe from them at all and they didn't make me feel like they really cared that much. They were a big brand – but that didn't bother me. I'm a very instinctive person and if I don't get the right feeling about something or someone then I won't want to do it. Even if it is a big opportunity. I won't put my name to something just for the money. It has to feel true to who I am. I probably made it pretty obvious how I felt because I kept getting up to go to the loo to be sick. I'm sure they left the room thinking I was extremely weird. Afterwards I said to Adam, 'I don't care that they're a big successful brand. The money isn't important to me. What matters is that it feels right.' Adam knows what I'm like and he told me it was entirely my call. But he said I should wait until I'd met the next people before I made any decision.

My next meeting was with a guy called Adam Frisby, from In The Style. I warmed to him instantly. He was really sweet and unassuming, and came into the room armed with a mood board that he and his team had made, with images and words about what I represented and why they wanted to work with me. He told me he thought I was a great role model to young girls, and that he loved my authenticity. He said I was the true definition of girl power, female positivity and an all-round girls' girl. He told me, 'You encompass everything that is great about modern women: funny, kind, loyal, driven and determined, showing you don't have to compromise on your values to be adored — we're the perfect fit as this is everything I have tried to make my brand stand for.' It was all so lovely and heartfelt, that I actually choked up a bit because I was so touched. He was the complete opposite of the last people, and when he told me how he'd come from nothing and had built the company through borrowing money and pure passion, I wanted to sign with him on the spot. He seemed to really understand my style and showed me loads of outfit designs he thought would work for me based on things I'd worn in *Love Island*. He also said that he envisaged the range being inclusive and suiting all sizes and shapes, which really hit home for me. I think EVERY girl needs to feel special in clothes.

The previous brand (I don't want to name and shame them, so won't say who they are) had provided me with outfits before and the sizes were way off, which made me feel like shit, because they made me feel bigger than I actually was. I told Adam I wanted people to feel great about themselves, not self-conscious. When sizes aren't right for you it really damages your body confidence, and I didn't want to be associated with anything that made girls feel awful.

'I think EVERY girl needs to feel special in clothes'

DRESS TO SUIT YOUR SHAPE

I'm lucky enough these days to have a stylist who helps me get ready for big events and TV shows. She's called Ellis Ranson and is great at knowing what suits me. She's also brilliant at knowing what works for different body shapes so I've asked her to share her secrets and tips here:

1. *IF YOU ARE CURVY WITH A TINY WAIST THEN YOU ARE AN HOURGLASS SHAPE.* Your goal is to highlight this shape, wearing belts round the waist or anything that ties you in. It won't make you look bigger; it will just give emphasis to your best asset! For the more brave, crop tops and pencil skirts are a great look for this body type. The perfect dress is the wrap; it holds you in at the waist and is mid length to cover the legs.

2. *IF YOU HAVE A SLIM BODY BUT CARRY WEIGHT AROUND YOUR MIDDLE,* then your aim is to highlight your shoulders and your legs. Anything high-waisted is good for you, as this will meet the torso at just the right spot to give

you shape that maybe you don't have. Bardot-style shift dresses are also great for showing off those collarbones. If you are shorter, take up the hem of your dress or skirt so you are showing off more leg – but not too short!

3. *IF YOU ARE BOTTOM HEAVY WITH A SMALLER TOP HALF THEN YOU ARE A PEAR*; you need to take attention away from your lower body, and bare shoulders is a great way to do this. A strong jacket will also do the trick of balancing out your shape. And a slim flare, which is very on trend, is another great way as they draw the eyes away from the hips making them seem perfectly proportioned.

4. *IF YOU HAVE SMALL BOOBS* take advantage of your flat chest as it means you have the pick of the bunch when it comes to shopping and fashion! Wear backless styles to show off more skin and cover up your chest, and with your back out looking sexy no one will even have a chance to consider your chest size. On the other hand don't be scared of plunging necklines as it can look very model-esque, plus you can add dainty layered necklaces to distract and highlight the collarbone.

Invest in a Wonderbra as they really do what the name says! Things to remember: crop tops, ribbed camis and oversized vest tops can be your wardrobe staples as they draw more attention to your arms and body and divert from the chest.

5. *IF YOU HAVE A BIGGER CHEST (EG A D+)* it can be quite difficult to find outfits that fit you without putting your chest completely on display or making you look larger than you are. The best advice is to create the hourglass figure to show off your waist and enhance the bust – don't hide it! But avoid any fuss or frills on the chest area, keep it simple. Sleeves and V necks are great for balance. Top tip: if you want to wear a blazer go up a size and get a dry-cleaner (your new best mate!) to alter it to fit you.

And find a style icon who has the same body shape as you and shamelessly copy her!

What Would Dani Do?

♡

How do you survive a WHOLE night in heels? I last 1 hour before the flats come out

Laura, 23, Croydon

Easy answer: I take two Nurofen before I go out!

What Would Dani Do?

♡

I'm going to a party and my ex will be there. What sort of outfit is guaranteed to make him regret ever dumping me? (P.S. I'm quite short and have no boobs.)

@Jodielee11

Jodie, 19, Manchester

Something classy. You can turn up and look all sexy with your boobs out but that's not going to make him regret being with you. Think about something more sophisticated, something that shows your back, and put some highlighter on your collarbone.

I'm not suddenly going to pretend I'm a fashion designer – for a start I'm shit at drawing – but from the minute I started working on my clothing range, it was always really important for me to be involved in as much of the detail as possible. I wanted to make sure the clothes were all things I genuinely loved and would want to wear and that everything had my stamp on it. So, I'd meet with the design team every couple of weeks and they would show me ideas based on stuff I liked, or things I'd described to them. I'd then add my own tweaks or colour changes, scribbling on the pictures they'd brought with them. Then they would draw up a new board of ideas for the next meeting, and make more suggestions for amendments, like which font to use on the slogan T-shirts or which material I liked and disliked. I told them I wouldn't wear up-the-arse dresses or anything 'too tight' or unflattering. Choosing the fabrics was a big deal for me, because I can't stand silky stuff – it makes me feel all weird. Someone sent me some really expensive silk pyjamas the other day and I had to give them away. I can't stand the feeling on my Nunnie. It's dead slimy when you put it on and gives me the heebie jeebies!

DANI'S DESIGN DOS AND DONT'S

· Don't put silk anywhere near me.

· I love cosy jumpers but not woollen knitwear – it makes me itch.

· Nothing clingy around the neck!

· Don't have a dress or shorts that are too 'up your arse'. Why does anyone want to see what's up there?

· I hate those tight metallic skirts. You spend all night pulling them down.

· I personally don't think you should wear anything that shows your boobs too much. There's a difference between girls who just have big boobs and are dressing to suit their shape, and girls who are just wearing stuff to show off. Why give everything away like that? No need.

In the end, we came up with a range that genuinely felt like it worked for everyone – lovely little flowing dresses ranging from a size 4 to a 24 so whatever your shape you could feel beautiful. We designed cute little jumpers, oversized T-shirts that you could tie up, playsuits, some smarter dresses, co-ords, casual tracksuits, fake fur coats and jeans. I was very conscious of developing a range that would suit a wide range of people, which was hard to do because I know you will never please everyone. And then I obviously went into a massive panic in case everyone slated it!

What Would Dani Do?

♡

I have really massive hips and I hate my tummy – what sort of outfit would suit me for a date night?

A jumper dress, as that will cover up the bits you don't like and will emphasise your legs instead. Playsuits are really flattering too.

IT'S A SELL-OUT!

Twenty-four hours before my collection went live, we did a special promotion so people could get the clothes early. Never for a second did I expect it to get the reaction it did. We had over 80,000 sign ups and by the time we had the launch party, 80% of the outfits had sold out!! Adam from In The Style was messaging me throughout the day with updates and neither of us could believe it – 'I haven't sold clothes like that for eight years!' he told me. I kept asking him if he was happy and he replied, 'Are you kidding, Dani? This

223

is incredible! It's surpassed all expectations I had. I always knew you would do well, but this is phenomenal – some of your styles were sold out within an hour!'

I was so chuffed. People can be your worst critic so there's no way they would buy the clothes if they didn't like them. At the launch party, I felt so proud because my mates were

all wearing outfits from the range and my mum and dad were there supporting me and were as overwhelmed as I was (either that or they were just pissed!). We had a catwalk in the middle of the event and I kept thinking, 'They're *my* clothes!'

I felt like Victoria Beckham. Well, the Canning Town version anyway.

IF CLOTHES COULD TALK

MY MOST MEMORABLE OUTFITS

- My 21st birthday outfit: it was white and off the shoulder and only cost me 12 quid from Missguided but I felt like a goddess. I felt good that day.

- My first premiere: it was for my film *We Still Kill the Old Way.* I wore a black dress that drooped at the back and had diamonds on it. I had never really dressed up that much before so I felt really special.

- The Pride of Britain Awards: I loved my dress for that; I felt like a princess. It was so long, glittery and elegant, and it really stood out. I didn't like it when I was walking about though, everyone kept treading on it and by the end of the night it was black at the bottom!

- Pyjamas: someone gave me a pair of black cotton ones with my initials on and I love them, they're so comfy. I would live in them if I could.

- The outfit I wore for the Radio One Teen Awards: it was a tight white dress that was really flattering and made me feel great. ✦

VOGUE CALLING!

I was asked to go and meet the editor of *Vogue* too! It was not long after I'd been out of *Love Island,* and I got invited to their offices in London. I kept thinking, 'What do they want with me?', and when I arrived, I saw a sea of beautiful creatures all really unique and different but all very tall. As I walked through their offices – dressed in a double denim skirt and a top, thinking, 'What will they make of this outfit?' – I could feel all these heads lifting up and looking at me. I sort of half-smiled, as if to say, 'What am I doing here? This is all very weird', and then I was told to sit in the waiting area. I was a bit intimidated at first, until someone came over and asked for a photo, and suddenly more and more of them came over and all started telling me how much they loved me on *Love Island* and they even complimented my outfit! Wow. What was going on?! When I met the editor, Edward Enninful, he was really lovely and warm, and we chatted about me doing some stuff for their website. It all went a bit over my head if I'm honest but I was just chuffed to be asked to come into *Vogue*. Anyway, I haven't heard back yet so I can't have impressed them that much. Maybe they just wanted some selfies!

What Would Dani Do?

I've lost 7 stone with @slimmingworld. How do I dress for my new and ever-changing body shape?

@antjess
Antje, 28, Windsor

Firstly – wow! Congratulations. And secondly this is a really great time to try out new styles and work out what suits you. Look at Instagram for inspiration and find people whose style and shapes you can relate to. Pick and mix things you fancy and start to work out what your individual style is. It's all about feeling body confident and trying things on, researching people, celebs you admire. Also when ordering stuff online don't worry about the sizing as it always comes up different in different stores – just try everything and have fun!

227

DANI'S TOP TEN WARDROBE MUST HAVES

1. *DEFINITELY AN ARIANA GRANDE-STYLE HOODY –* something really oversized that you can style with boots or chill on the sofa with.

2. *SLOGAN TEE –* I love a slogan tee; it's very day-to-night and can be styled down or popped with a going-out skirt for a night out.

3. *PAPER-BAG SKIRT –* I adore anything with a paper-bag waist, it's flattering for all shapes and sizes and something you can wear day or night again.

4. *DENIM JEANS (MOM FIT) –* my go-to outfit tends to be some mom-fit denim jeans and a nice shirt.

5. *PRINTED OVERSIZE SHIRT –* I love animal print shirts and they can be styled with jeans for the perfect casual but glam look.

6. *CO-ORD –* I love a cute two piece, as long as it's not an overpowering print. They're an easy go-to outfit.

7. *FRILL PLAYSUIT –* super cute but easy to wear and looks very flattering: perfect for a night out.

8. *WRAP DRESS –* this is a really easy day/night look. It's flattering for ALL sizes as it wraps over and has frills on.

9. *OVERSIZE JUMPER DRESS* (knitted) – perfect to throw on during winter (but I'm really picky when it comes to knitwear so it has to be non-itchy!).

10. *CROPPED SLOGAN JUMPER* – I loved the 'what time's your flight' slogan from my In The Style range because it was what Jack said to me on *Love Island* when we had the row. This teamed with some jeans or a paper-bag skirt is such a cute little day time outfit. Fun and girly.

What Would Dani Do?

I really don't like what my boyfriend wears - how can I help style him without offending him?

Ooh that's a good one. My mate Ellie will get the clothes out for her boyfriend and say, 'What do you think of this?' At the end of the day everyone has different taste so you shouldn't be one of those girlfriends who says 'wear this, wear that'. You don't want to insult him. Just give him ideas and be subtle about it. After all, you wouldn't like someone telling you what to wear, would you?

Chapter Ten

Keep Your Head On!

Some of the girls on *Love Island* would put on a full face of make-up just to step outside, which gave me a headache just to think about it. I was far too lazy. Plus, if I'm honest, I didn't really have a clue what I was doing when it came to putting on the slap. I would wear a bit of mascara and some BB cream when I went on dates with Jack, but I could never see the point in plastering it on just to sit round the pool! I think the others did it because they knew we were on telly, and wanted to look their best, but I didn't really care. I figured that the moment I started wearing it, then I'd have to do it all the time, and I'd end up in a big-dark-eyeliner-smudged-make-up-hole I couldn't get out of. I just couldn't be bothered. I thought, 'I know I'm on a TV show but I'm also just being myself so I'm not going to pretend I'm something I'm not.' So, while some of the other girls spent hours getting ready, I was outside baking myself in the sun. That's why I had the best tan. I used to sunbathe *all day*. The girls would wear fake tan instead and just sit in the shade – they didn't want to sunbathe and get all hot and sweaty. Me, on the other hand, would sweat like a pig then jump in the pool. Jack didn't sunbathe either but somehow, he was always more tanned than me. He just had to look at the sun and he darkened. Why is it that boys never have to put in so much effort?!

What Would Dani Do?

♡

How do you get such clear skin?

@ x_siennadawn_x
Sienna, 16

Proactiv is the best as they have something for every skin type. I follow their three-step system by using their exfoliating cleanser, then their face cream and finally their moisturiser. Also, never squeeze a spot – it can become a scar!

What Would Dani Do?

♡

How do you look after your skin and get your hair looking so shiny?

Serena, 30, London

1. Never sleep with make-up on

2. Always moisturise

3. Try a hair mask treatment once a week

DANI'S MAKE-UP MUSTS

The only things I am really fussy about are my fake eyelashes and my face cream.

1. ALWAYS CLEAN YOUR FACE!

I'm obsessed with keeping my skin healthy and I have a whole Proactiv routine that I've been doing for years. My mum made me go to a dermatologist for advice after I had a really bad breakout of spots on my forehead, and I stopped using face wipes after that because I found out they're bad for you and really dry your skin. I do sometimes still get spots but that's because I'm working

233

so much at the moment so I've constantly got make-up on – but I couldn't survive without my Proactiv products. I appreciate they might seem expensive in comparison to other options you can get, but they work so well for me that I consider them a brilliant investment; I might be their biggest fan! I'd quite like to get one of those chemical peels on my skin too (although they take a layer of your face off, so you can't go out for a few days afterwards just in case you start shedding like a snake!).

2. *LOOK AFTER YOUR LASHES*

I didn't realise that blow-drying my lashes would turn into such a big thing! I thought everyone did it, but apparently it caused a right storm back home and people thought I was really bizarre and weird. I've done it since I was 16 years old, ever since my lash lady, Nicky, told me it was a good way to keep them looking fresh. I used to have my lashes done every two and a half weeks (apart from when I was on *Love Island* and they went all clumpy) until I gave them a break recently. I don't think I could cope without them. I feel like, when you've got a bit of lash on, and you wake up in the morning, you think, 'I'm alright!', whereas without them, you feel naked and look like a bald chicken. Nicky gave me the tip about washing the lashes, and it's the best hack I know.

The trick is to try to avoid putting mascara on them because that's when they start falling out. But washing them gives them volume and makes them look brand new. And if you don't wash them, they can get all greasy looking because they're made of real hair. I use Johnson's Baby Shampoo once a day and it works a treat.

What Would Dani Do?

♡

If you could create your own make-up line what would you call it?

I'm lucky enough that I got the chance to bring out my own strip lash range with a brilliant Irish brand called SOSU, run by a really successful blogger called Suzanne Jackson – we've called it Girlcode! I'd also love a line that is all about skin, and products that make you glow. And I would have to create some sun protection lotion for the girls that are like me and love to sunbathe!

MY LOVE ISLAND ROUTINE

A.M.:

1. Eye mask off (this was not only good to keep Jack's hands at bay but it's good to keep your fake eyelashes tidy).

2. Have a coffee. One sugar or two sweeteners. Not too strong. I like those sachets that make lattes, except for when you get a lump in the bottom and it's like swallowing a bogey.

3. Shower and scrub my face with Proactiv exfoliator.

4. Dry my body, dry my face.

5. Apply Dermalogica sun cream.

P.M.:

1. Wash eyelashes: get a little dollop of Johnson's Baby Shampoo in the palm of my hand, get two fingers and rub them each individually. Rinse it with water and then brush with an eyelash brush and dry, not too hot though or it'll burn your face.

2. Slap on a bit of BB cream, which is like a tinted moisturiser and doesn't feel like you've caked anything on.

3. If one of the girls would do it for me: eyeliner and some eyeshadow.

4. Then before bed: Proactiv scrub, then Dermalogica cleanser with cotton pads and then Proactiv facial cream.

What Would Dani Do?

♡

How do you do you manage to get your hair looking lovely? I've tried to get my hair looking nice but it always fails!

@emilyprincesswalton

Emily, 24, Cambridgeshire

It's all about finding the right shampoo and conditioner and also doing a hair mask once a week. Since leaving the villa I get my hair styled pretty much every day when I am on a job so looking after it is a must. I use Redken to wash and condition, and use a Kérastase hair mask (the one in the green pot!).

(Top tip: If your hair gets backcombed for a particular style, NEVER try and brush it out, it will break your hair. Wait until you can have a shower and wash your hair with lots of conditioner!)

LET YOUR HAIR DOWN

The only downside of sitting about in the sun all the time was the fact that my hair went ginger! I kept trying to make it darker with brown shampoo but it just made it look like someone had gone at me with a felt tip pen. My natural hair colour is mousey brown, although I bleached it bright blonde once when I was younger, which made me look like a ball of hay. It started breaking off and was the worst condition it's ever been in my life. Nowadays I have it dyed a chocolate-brown. In the winter I like to go a bit darker and in the summer, I will have a bit of ombré so it's lighter at the ends. I love having long hair so I've always had hair extensions because my hair's quite short underneath. Ariana Grande is my Hair Idol because her ponytail looks like a horse's tail whipping about onstage – it's just so shiny and perfect. Me and Jack went to watch her in concert recently, and he was obsessed with her hair. He kept saying, 'Her hair is incredible!' Eventually I got pissed off and shouted, 'It's extensions, you know, Jack!'

I was so chuffed when I was asked to sign up to Mark Hill to be a hair ambassador for him. I think the brand wanted to work with me because I am hair-obsessed, plus I have the sort of followers who would buy their products. I guess that because I'm a normal girl it meant I could genuinely learn how to use the range and talk about it in a way that was relatable. I would never pretend I could do something or wear something if it wasn't authentic and true to me. I never used to have a clue about hair wands – I thought there was only one type of curler and that was that. I didn't realise you could get them in all shapes and sizes! But it was when I was doing *Nativity!* that the brand really changed my life. I had

to do my own hair and make-up and was really panicking that I would look a mess, so Mark Hill sent me heated rollers to use because they were super easy. And now I don't think I will ever look back. I bloody love them!

DANI'S HAIR HACKS

1. *KEEP IT IN GOOD CONDITION* – you should put treatments on your hair at least once a week because it really does make a difference. I put a hair mask on last night and it really helped; I'm stroking it now and it feels lovely!

2. *DON'T WASH YOUR HAIR TOO OFTEN.* The more you wash it, the more you need to wash it. I only do mine once or twice a week. If you get a greasy fringe just wash that bit on its own in between!

3. *GIVE YOUR HAIR A DAY OFF.* Imagine constantly getting pulled about and backcombed and sprayed with hairspray?! Your poor hair needs a break sometimes just like you do.

4. *ALWAYS USE A HEAT PROTECTOR* to make sure you don't damage the hair.

5. *I AM A MASSIVE FAN OF THE LOOSE-WAVES LOOK* so use a medium-size tong and curl the hair in different directions for a more 'beachy' style.

MAKE IT – DON'T FAKE IT

My idea of make-up used to be foundation that finished on my chin because I didn't realise you had to work it into the neckline. I'm also pretty shit at applying eyeshadow; I don't know how to blend, so my attempt at a smoky eye usually looks more like someone has punched me in the head. And don't even get me started on contouring. What is that even about? It's like someone has completely changed your face and turned you into Barbie. Some girls will look at a highlighter and it will give them palpitations because they are so excited by it, but not me. Until recently I thought a highlighter was just a pen you got in WHSmith.

These days I'm lucky enough to have someone to do my make-up for me when needed, which is brilliant. But it also means I've become even lazier (and more impatient!) when I'm at home and left to do it myself.

'I thought a highlighter was just a pen you got in WHSmith'

So, thank the lord for Marcos Gurgel. He's now my official hair and make-up artist and I am fully addicted to him. I met him when he did my make-up for the final episode of *Love Island Aftersun* and I have been in love with him ever since. I would be so happy if he just agreed to move in with me so I never have to do my own face again. I've had make-up artists who have plastered me in so much slap that I barely recognised myself, but Marcos somehow manages to make me look really natural yet loads prettier! When he did my make-up for *Aftersun* people told me that it was the best I had ever looked. And he made my eyes really pop out, which I loved.

DANI'S MAKE-UP ESSENTIALS (AS DIRECTED BY MARCOS!)

- One of those Beauty Blender blending sponge things. Marcos taught me to use it for my foundation and they're so much better than fingers or a brush! Giorgio Armani Luminous Silk Foundation is my go-to as it has enough coverage but never leaves me looking cakey.

- I love glowy skin so I have been adding a couple of drops of liquid highlighter to my foundation and mixing them up before application.

- I also use NARS concealers. Marcos got me into them as they cover those dark circles in no time but still make me look like me.

- A cream bronzer by Chanel called Soleil Tan De Chanel. Marcos has taught me that you put it on all the same places where the sun would get you so your nose, your chin, the outside portion of your face.

- Bobbi Brown cream blusher pots – I put it on the apples of my cheeks and blend with my fingers! The idea is that I am blushing from within!

- I love glossy lips! My fave is Gloss Bomb by Rihanna's Fenty Beauty. It makes your lips look 'wet' plus it plumps them up.

- Although I get my brows microbladed, Marcos still fills them in with a HD Brows pencil for a sharper look.

MARCOS ON BUDGET BEAUTY BUYS:

Although I am lucky enough to get sent all these amazing make-up products to try out and use on my clients, I also love going to high-street chemists and finding 'cheaper make-up' that performs just as well as the more expensive brands.

Here are some of my hidden gems . . .

- Maybelline Super Stay 24hr Lip Colour – this lipstick will last you all day and it won't leave your lips feeling dry.

- Bourjois Healthy Mix Foundation – hands down one of my favourite high street foundations. It reminds me of Chanel's Vitalumière.

· Mascara is where you can really save you hard-earned cash. High street mascaras are in my opinion better than high end ones. There are loads of them out there you just have to find the one that suits you!

*

Girls always notice if I do something funny to my face or wear too much make-up and they will comment on Instagram saying it doesn't look like me. So it's great to have Marcos, because he knows what suits me and what I like. He says I wouldn't look right having my face contoured because that's a different type of 'Instagram girl', which isn't me.

While we're on the subject of 'no bullshit', I've decided that, rather than me telling you how to do your make-up, I will to pass you over to Marcos the master himself. Because he's the one who knows what he's talking about.

MARCOS ON DANI:

As a make-up artist, there are faces that you look at and think, "I would love to do her make-up", and that's how I felt about Dani because not only did she seem really nice but her face is really lovely and she's got my kind of style. The first time I did Dani's make-up, I was inspired to create a glam version of the Dani Dyer I saw on *Love Island*. I knew she liked minimal make-up and preferred to look natural but as she was a guest on a TV show she still needed to look a bit special. So, for *Love Island Aftersun* I set about creating a Golden Goddess version of her *Love Island* self. Then for shows like *Celebrity Juice* when it was their 10th anniversary I used glitter and made her more glam but still fun because it was a celebration and a party – and she loved it.

MARCOS' TOP MAKE-UP TIPS

1. ALWAYS USE A PRIMER

Primers are really important when setting the face. They help prolong the make-up and absorb the oil. If you want your face of make-up to hold, don't forget to prime! And it's not just one-type-fits-all either. There is a face primer that primes your foundation and keeps it from getting all dry and looking patchy. And there's an eye primer that will absorb the oil and stop your eyeshadow creasing.

2. TRY, TRY, TRY BEFORE YOU BUY YOUR FOUNDATION

Never buy a foundation just because people say it's amazing. Go to a counter and try a patch on your skin, then go outside and take a mirror with you. This is the harshest light and the light you need to see it in. Ask yourself, does it suit you? Is the colour matching? And does it look natural? Don't just have the same foundation for 12 months either. Your skin will get darker in the summer so you need to match your foundation with the seasons. If you look back at *Love Island* 2017, at one point Montana had a very pale face because she only had that one foundation she used all year round.

3. YOUR EYESHADOW SHOULD BE THE OPPOSITE OF YOUR EYE COLOUR

When it comes to picking a great eyeshadow, you should look at a colour wheel or a colour chart like you get with paints in IKEA or B&Q. Look at your eye colour and then see what's the opposite to that colour – that will really make your eyes pop. Which is why purple will always go well with green eyes, orangey colours will always go with blue eyes and blue tones are beautiful for brown eyes. Sometimes your eyes will have a hint of another colour in them too so make sure you consider this – Dani has a hint of green in her eyes so that means I can also blend an element of purple sometimes.

4. PICK OUT THE COLOUR OF YOUR CLOTHES

It's never a good idea to go all matchy-matchy with your eyeshadow and a dress because you will look like a clown. But there are ways to make your outfit and face stand out more. If Dani was wearing a pink dress I wouldn't give her pink eyeshadow and a pink lip because she would look dead, so instead I would pick out hues of that colour, subtle glimmers of pink within a blusher or eyeshadow that make it all pop.

5. EYEBROWS ARE SISTERS NOT TWINS

The best lesson you can learn about your brows is that they are sisters and not twins. No face is symmetrical, so they will never be the same as each other unless you draw them in and then it becomes fake-looking like 'the Instagram brow'. So, look after them and shape them, but don't try and make them the perfect match. Just the shape of your brow can change your face in a really clever way – Dani has had hers microbladed to add a higher arch, which has really opened up her eyes. Some people comment they think she's had work done but it's just make-up tricks!

6. DON'T DO IT ALL

If you're making more of your eyes then leave the lips subtler and vice versa. The ultimate goal is for people to see you and say, 'Oh my God, you look lovely!', instead of 'Oh my God, I love your make-up!' So, don't change your face, embrace who you are.

DANI'S BEST FEATURES (BY MARCOS!)

1. Her eyes – they are mesmerizing. She had a real striking look and that's a dream for any make-up artist plus she

has plenty of eye space for the eyeshadows that I use (never less than five shades to create that smoky effect).

2. I adore her skin, I could actually not use any foundation just moisturiser! She really looks after her skin.

3. Although she has plumped her lips previously like Kylie Jenner, Dani has naturally beautiful lips anyway and they suit any shade from nude to reds (especially orange shades; I love an orange lip!).

Chapter Eleven

The Fame Game

What Would Dani Do?

♡

I want to be famous . . . Is it as good and fun as it looks?

I think fame is good in different ways but it depends how you use it, if you know what I mean. Fame is great as it can give you many lovely things and so many opportunities, but it also means you have to give up certain privileges that you take for granted, like hanging out and being normal with your mates, or going on a girly holiday. It's crazy because you can end up getting paranoid that someone is always looking at you! Some people went on Love Island to be famous, but that wasn't really the case for me; I've always wanted to be in the limelight, but mainly because I love acting and knew this would be a great platform to help that. So, as amazing as fame is, it also means you have to constantly have your guard up, as you worry that people are waiting for you to say something wrong. But maybe that's just me. Perhaps I'm a little bit too cautious with everything . . .

HOW TO KEEP YOUR FEET ON THE GROUND AND NOT LET FAME GO TO YOUR HEAD

1. DON'T GET TOO PISSED (OR STAY OUT TOO LATE!)

I'm not someone who loves staying out late anyway – give me my slippers over stilettos any day! – but now I'm in the public eye, I feel like staying out until 3 a.m. can be risky because if I was pissed, I could say the wrong thing to the wrong person. I know it sounds terrible, but I feel like I don't know who to trust when I'm out. I have been in a situation where someone came up to me and started asking me questions about how me and Jack were, and I thought she was just a normal girl, then

☆

she dropped in that she was a journalist! I've come to the conclusion I'm better off getting drunk indoors with my mates where I know I'll be safe!

2. . . . AND DON'T GET HANGOVERS

Another reason not to get too smashed is because you have to be up early for work and you need to look good and act professional! If I'd gone out boozing all the time I'd never have been able to do the breakfast show on Capital FM or make an appearance on morning TV. Alcohol is a depressant, and in the career I'm in at the minute, I can't afford to be getting hungover because I need to get up, be on form and do things – and be in a good mood!

3. TREAT EVERY OPPORTUNITY LIKE IT'S YOUR LAST ONE

Having a famous dad has meant I'm more clued up and aware of the ups and downs of fame. So, I know how easily everything could disappear. I'm lucky because I know I want to act but for others, like Jack, who have come from normal jobs, I think it can be a really tough adjustment. Jack might want to go back to selling pens but I don't think he can any more because too many people know who he is. Yet on the other hand, he doesn't yet know exactly what he wants to do or where he wants to land in life. So it's important to look at every opportunity we get and think about how that can help us in the future and what sort of career path it might lead to.

4. *DON'T TAKE OTHER PEOPLE FOR GRANTED*

My dad has always said to me, 'Never treat anyone you meet any differently. If you're on set that means everyone from the directors, the cameramen, the runners, the make-up artists and the cleaners should be the same. You need all of them as much as they need you.' And that applies to people you meet on the street. He's taught me to always be considerate of others. He's a really kind person and has always had time for his fans. It's difficult sometimes now if he's with my little brother Arty, and someone asks for a picture, but he does try his best to treat them all with equal respect.

'Never treat people any differently – from the directors to the cleaners. You need all of them as much as they need you'

5. *LISTEN TO THE ADVICE OF THOSE WHO HAVE BEEN THERE*

Again, I'm lucky to have my dad who has been there and done that. So, he tells me what to look out for and helps guide me. Jack doesn't have that, so I try and help him myself. He doesn't listen as much as I want him to so when tell him, 'Jack, I know how it works', he says, 'But how do you know about it? I was a winner the same as you!'

☆

6. BE YOUR OWN PERSON

As much as I love the fact I'm in a couple with Jack and we were on the same journey together, I also know it's important to do my own thing and take jobs that don't involve him. I adore my dad and the fact that now I'm being offered the chance to work with him on things like *Gogglebox* and *Nativity! The Musical* is a dream come true. To have that opportunity is all I've ever wanted so I'm not going to turn down anything that I really want to do. I've learnt to be strong and know my own mind and stick to my guns.

MY FIRST TASTE OF FAME

Landing at Stansted Airport the day after the *Love Island* final was one of the nuttiest and craziest experiences of my life. I have honestly never seen anything like it in my life, apart from in films. As soon as we came through the doors in the airport, we heard this huge deafening cheer and I looked out to a sea of faces all staring at us, some with banners, others crying, people screaming and shouting our names. Our friends and family were among the crowd waiting for us, but most of the people there were just fans of *Love Island*. People we had never seen before in our entire lives! They were going berserk. People were asking for our autographs and there were photographers everywhere. It was really intense. I had no idea it was going to be like that.

When I got asked for my autograph I didn't know what to do! I didn't have a proper one worked out. How was I meant to write my name? I'd only ever done my signature in the bank before! I wasn't prepared for this! 'Can I have a hug?' 'Can I have a picture?' 'Can you say hello to my little sister?' There were all these strangers queuing up to say hello to me. Yet, even though it was overwhelming, I knew from my dad how important it was to give people my time. It's not fair when famous people treat their fans badly.

I should know . . . it happened to me . . .

*

NEVER MEET YOUR IDOLS!

What Would Dani Do?

♡

Who's your biggest idol? Who have you had a fan girl moment over?

There's one boy I had a crush on BADLY.
And I definitely wasn't alone in my obsession.

He was the first boy I ever fancied. I was 13 at the time, and I remember lying on my bed gazing up at my wall, plastered with pictures of his face that I'd printed off the Internet and stuck up delicately with Blu Tack. In one shot he had a cap on, and you could see his floppy hair poking out, and I thought he was sooooo fit. I would sit and daydream about what life would be like when we got married (because that was obviously going to happen); we would live in his plush pad in Hollywood and everyone would say what a perfect couple we were. I remember saying – to anyone who would listen – 'I will *never ever* divorce him.' We would always be together.

'Mr and Mrs Dani and Justin Bieber.'

I'd never fancied a boy the way I fancied Justin. It was like the first time you've ever tasted a Chinese. You know when you taste something so good and can't believe you have never had it before? Falling in love with Justin Bieber was like tasting my first duck roll.

'Falling in love with Justin Bieber was like tasting my first duck roll'

Somehow, I managed to convince my parents to let me bunk off school for the day to go and meet him at a signing in HMV Westfield in Shepherd's Bush. This was the one of the first times he'd come over to the UK, and it was a *big* deal. He wasn't all buff and muscular like he is now (even my mum has a calendar of him on her wall these days!); this was back when he was scrawny and skinny and it was all about the hair flick. Remember the video for his song 'Baby' when he stood there on the roundabout with that long lovely hair falling in his face? DREAMY! I like to think I was one of the first Beliebers, because I discovered him on YouTube, and me and my mate, Daisy, would spend hours watching him and dissecting his every move. Just like every other teenage girl on the planet, I fell head over hair in love with him.

How the hell I persuaded Mum and Dad to let me take the day off school I'll never know. They were usually quite strict about that sort of stuff. I think I told them I didn't have any 'proper' lessons that day. 'Go on,' I pleaded, 'just say I'm ill, let me have this one day off!' I really turned the charm on. I was a good kid in school, so it's terrible when I think about it now. My mum found it quite amusing and dad thought it was a harmless infatuation even though he thought Justin was 'a bit of a weapon with weird hair'.

We had to get there for 5 a.m. Daisy stayed over at mine the night before and neither of us could sleep a wink. We were so excited. Dad had agreed to drive us there. He was wearing his grandad cap (which he always wears if he goes out in the morning because he hasn't done his hair properly) and when we arrived, it was still pitch-black. Dad dropped us off at the park point and we had to walk to the main entrance about five minutes away. He said, 'Go on then, go do what you gotta do', and smiled. 'I'll wait in the car park so make sure you ring me once you've got a ticket.' We got to Westfield and there were people camping out overnight! The tickets weren't guaranteed so there was a chance we could have turned up and been sent away. But two hours later, and we finally got what we came for . . . we were in! Only problem was, Justin wasn't due to be there until 5 p.m. that evening, so we had more than a few hours to kill. We went to Sainsbury's and got all our little foods for the day – tuna pasta, crisps, chocolate and some other bits. We didn't have much money so we couldn't exactly go on a shopping spree, but we went to Accessorize and bought a couple of bracelets and then to Boots and got a cheapy foundation from Barry M. I bloody loved me a bit of Barry M.

When it got to 4 p.m., we were told we all had to re-queue. Me and Daisy rushed through to the front – there was no way we were queueing again for another two hours. Justin's song 'Favourite Girl' was blaring out of the speakers and it gave me goosebumps.

Justin arrived and was ushered through to the store. He was surrounded by bouncers so I could hardly see him among the crowd but the atmosphere was nuts. People were screaming and sobbing, 'My God, it's Justin Bieber!' I was getting myself psyched up; this was my big moment . . . this was when I would somehow convince him to marry me. I honestly thought we were going to have a chat and get to know each other. I remember everything about that moment like it was yesterday: the music was playing quite dimly; my heart was beating so fast; I could see him in front of us at the desk with all his albums piled up, and I had a piece of paper in my hand with my phone number on! I was thinking, 'If we have a chat I can just slip it in his hand.' It wasn't that I was really confident; it was more that I knew this was my only chance and I didn't want to blow it. And surely there was no reason why I couldn't convince Justin Bieber that we were meant to be together? Daisy went ahead of me, and I noticed he wasn't really looking at anyone; he just seemed really distracted like he wasn't really there. Then it was my turn. I was so shaky, I was petrified. I clutched my little screwed-up number in my hand and suddenly . . .

. . . it was over.

He didn't even look up when he scribbled his name on my copy of his album! It all went so quickly, like I was on a conveyor belt. I don't feel like I even stopped; I was being ushered past him so speedily that the next person was in my place within seconds. Justin's head was down the whole time and he was throwing his albums at people as if they were empty crisp packets. Like it all meant nothing.

LIKE I MEANT NOTHING.

He didn't even look at me.

I was so disappointed.

Dad was outside waiting and I burst into tears. I couldn't believe it. He said, 'Babe, what do you expect? This is why I say you should never meet your idols.'

And his words have rung in my ears ever since.

CAN I HAVE A SELFIE?

Dad jokes that I'm more famous than him now. I used to be the one who would always be asked to take the photo when his fans came over to him, and now it's the other way round! I still have to pinch myself to think there are that many people wanting to know what I'm up to. I can't bring myself to call them fans either because it sounds really cringe. I am so grateful that people have supported me – it means the absolute world – but 'fans'? What have I done to deserve that? I haven't saved anyone's life!

It was even more mad when I found out I had some famous followers!

When I came out of the villa and got my phone back, the messages I got were insane. I still haven't managed to reply to all of them (and it's probably a little bit too late now to say thank you!). The absolute best one I got was a DM from Millie Bobby Brown who plays Eleven in *Stranger Things*. I am OBSESSED with that show! She wrote, 'Oh my God, I love you, I want to meet you!', and I nearly fell over. What the fuck? I thought, 'Why do you want to meet me, you talented little bastard?!' She's British and is actually from round my way, but she lives in the States these days.

To think that she had found time to watch *Love Island* in the middle of her busy schedule! She told me she would love to go for lunch and gave me her American mobile number. I messaged her back to say thank you, and that I thought she was so, so talented. I'd love to go for lunch with her but it would be weird, wouldn't it?! I told her to get in touch when she's next in London and I'll take my little sister to meet her.

IN MY HEAD?

I suffer from something called sleep paralysis. It's the scariest thing ever; you're lying in bed as if you're asleep and your body can't move but your brain is fully awake. You get it from lack of sleep, stress and anxiety and it's awful. I've looked it up on Google before, which is the worst thing you can do because you will just end up thinking you're about to die. If you've sprained your ankle you'll come off the Internet thinking you need your foot amputated, and if you've got a headache then you've probably got a brain tumour! But sleep paralysis is a horrible thing to have, and being in the public eye only seems to make it worse. I know I shouldn't but I sometimes lie in bed worrying about what story is going to be in the papers about me the next day or if the paps have taken a horrible picture.

When we came out of *Love Island* they followed me and Jack everywhere. I think they wanted to get the first shot of him meeting my dad so they chased us all over London, and every time they took a set of pictures they would run stories that just made me feel like shit. My dad has always told me not to read the papers, because he says you will only focus on the bad stuff rather than anything good and it will bring you down. He gets upset by negative stories and comments but he's learnt now not to bite back. He used to flip out and fight back over every negative comment but he got to the point where he realised he wasn't appreciating the nice things people said about him. Now he says he's more bothered about saying thank you to the people who really do love him and support him.

My mum is the best role model when it comes to ignoring all the haters. She just seems to bat it all away. She has had to put up with so much shit being with my dad – especially because other women love him so much. Someone even set up a Facebook group once dedicated to talking about the fact that mum wasn't good enough to be with my dad! How mean is that?! Somehow, she just ignores it all.

BRAIN DRAIN

The anxiety I got when I was younger has gotten worse since being in the public eye too. Although going to therapy when I was 16 helped me to deal with some of it, there are still days when it creeps right back in. I think I have always had anxiety, but didn't realise before what it was. My mum and dad know when it's kicking in, by the way I'm behaving, and they can always help me out of it and pull me back. But nowadays I'm not with them as much, so I have to deal with it on my own. And it's hard because I don't want to talk openly about it, which means people just think I'm moody or being weird.

I had one attack after my In The Style launch party back in October 2018, and that's when I had to cancel a PA in Birmingham. I woke up the morning after the party and just felt totally shit. I can't explain it, because I wasn't remotely hungover. I just felt rubbish and I couldn't face the crowds. I was really suffering with going out on my own – something that still bothers me now – and I was anxious about being in a PA situation like that, in a shopping centre, because of the number of people who would be around. I also didn't want anyone seeing me if I wasn't at my best. I'm not one of those people who can be fake and turn on the smiles if something's not right in my head, and I simply wasn't in a good frame of mind.

So, I pulled out of the appearance.

This was on the Friday, and the following day I was due to fly to Spain to meet my best mate Kayleigh; we'd booked it months earlier, so it didn't even occur to me not to go. I needed a break and some time to be normal.

But I forgot that I'm not normal any more . . . and I can't do the things I used to do.

I got to the airport and it suddenly hit me – hard. I was on my own, and I could see people staring at me. I looked down at the floor and pulled my cap over my face. I really felt at that moment like I couldn't handle it. The woman at the check-in desk started being really rude and abrupt to me, and I felt my jaw wobbling. I had tears in my eyes and wanted to just burst out crying but I knew I couldn't. I was getting really anxious and panicky because people were looking at me and I couldn't even let out how I was feeling. My mind was all over the shop.

As I got to passport control, the pressure in my head was getting worse. It was like a vice on my brain. I could feel a big group of girls looking at me. They were on a hen party, and one of them was screaming, 'Is that Dani Dyer?' Then one of them tapped me on the shoulder and said, 'Can you wait there for us to come through so we can have a photo?'

I wanted to say yes. As I said before, I know how important it is to have photos with people who ask you, and that you should be nice to everyone you meet. But my brain was whirring and my head felt tight. It was as if I was going to faint. And I knew if I stopped for them, then all the other people who had been looking at me would also ask for a picture. I just wasn't in the right mindset.

I looked at her.

'I'm sorry, I can't.'

I rushed through without looking behind me. I knew I'd disappointed them, but I couldn't help it.

I had a momentary flashback to the time I met Justin Bieber. Not that I was ever comparing my experience to his level of fame, but I kind of understood a bit more about what he must have been going through and the reasons why he maybe wasn't as 'up for it' as I had hoped he would be. I was convinced I wouldn't ever be rude to people who come up to me but sometimes circumstances have meant that I have been 'off' and I feel bad about it. But at the same time I hope people can understand that I have bad days when I look or feel rubbish and I'm not the person people expect me to be.

When I arrived in Spain, I was so glad to see Kayleigh. I gave her a massive hug. It was like I'd come home. We slept in a single bed together. I didn't even get drunk; we just spent the days sat on the beach listening to music. It was just what I needed to feel more like me again. Without thinking, I posted a picture on Instagram of myself in the sun.

The comments flooded in. 'Why are you so selfish going on holiday instead of meeting your fans?' Loads of people were hurling abuse at me telling me that my 'five minutes of fame is up!' and that everything had gone to my head. They were telling me how I'd let people down, and that I wasn't who they thought I was. I recognised one of the messages as one of the girls who I didn't get a photo with. Was that a mistake? What had I done? I felt awful and so sad. I had to post a response.

I wrote, 'I make time for everyone and sometimes I need time for myself and my friend. Please understand that. I don't ever cancel anything unless I really can't attend something. So, don't judge PLEASE!!''

But they still kept coming, and it got so bad I had to turn the comments off at one point, because reading them was upsetting me so much. I didn't want to be one of those people who let others down. I have never cancelled anything in my life, this wasn't me. I didn't want people to hate me for it.

People genuinely seemed to think I'd ducked out of the appearance to go on holiday instead. But because it had been booked ages ago, it had never occurred to me to cancel.

SOME WAYS TO COPE WHEN ANXIETY CREEPS IN

1. Listen and breathe. There's an app called Calm that really helps me focus and take a step back from my whirring brain.

2. Ask yourself what exactly it is you're worried about – is it really going to happen and does worrying actually help?

3. How much does it really matter?

4. Can you actually change any of it by worrying so much?

5. What is there in your life that has happened that you should be grateful for? Think about this instead of the stuff that hasn't even happened yet.

6. Listen to music.

7. Read a really good book.

8. Watch your favourite TV show.

9. Exercise.

10. Talk to someone – for me it's my dad because he's like my comfort blanket and knows exactly how to reason with me and calm me down. So find someone close you can trust. If not, there is no shame in speaking to your doctor and asking to be referred to someone – loads of people go to therapy these days. It's totally normal. It's sometimes great to offload to someone who knows nothing about you.

THE PERKS!

I'm not going to be a complete Debbie Downer though. There are plenty of totally brilliant things about being in the public eye – especially the fantasic gifts! Ever since I came out of *Love Island* the sort of stuff I've been sent is ridiculous. If I so much as mention something on social media it's sent to me. Like Laura Mercier face creams; when they arrived, I shrieked, 'Are you kidding me? They are so expensive!' I've been sent amazing bags, clothes, hair stuff and bits for my flat. But far the best stuff?

My cleaning products.

There's a Spanish brand called Nenuco that I've used since I was little, because of my holidays to Majorca with Nan and Bruv, and I love it. I talked about it once on Twitter and now they've basically sent me everything from the factory! There's this stuff you bathe with, which is like an oil that has zero chemicals in and makes your skin feel incredible. They've also sent me washing powder, soap, washing-up liquid, floor cleaner, toilet drops, plug ins – the lot. Forget designer shoes – it's all about Nenuco!

268

I'M ON THE TELLY!

It's always been my dream to do stuff with my dad, and now we're in a position where we get asked to be guests on the same TV shows or red-carpet events.

We were both asked to be in the theatre production of *Nativity! The Musical* over Christmas. Dad plays a Hollywood producer and I am his daughter, Polly Parker, an aspiring actress who also works as one of his assistants. After Mr Maddens fails to persuade the Hollywood studio head to go to Coventry to watch their school nativity, Polly pleads with her father to give him and the children a chance. Having been so wrapped up in his work he has forgotten the joy that Christmas brings and is reminded through his daughter what Christmas is all about.

We had such a laugh performing together. Doing stuff with my dad just doesn't ever feel like work. I love being on telly with him too. Dad's been on *Celebrity Juice* loads of times before, so when he was asked to appear alongside me and Jack he knew it would be funny – he just told me and Jack to have a laugh and not worry about whatever Keith Lemon said to us because, 'The more you bite back or react to him, the more he keeps going and deliberately winds you up!' Jack was shitting himself; he was so nervous about what Keith was going to say to him that he downed a few beers. I think we got off quite lightly in the end, apart from the fact that Keith made my dad do a Mr & Mrs-style quiz with us, and read out questions like, 'How long does it take before Jack shoots his load in the bedroom?' My dad was cringing but laughing at the same time. Jack replied, 'Five minutes' – which, to be fair, was at least honest! Keith was lovely behind the scenes, and in between takes he kept asking, 'Are you alright?' He only wants to make a fun show and have a laugh with you.

One of my proudest moments was standing on the red carpet with my dad at the TV Choice Awards in 2018. *Love Island* was nominated (we didn't win, but never mind) and my dad was also nominated for Best Soap Actor. He completely deserved to win his category and I felt so honoured to be there watching him. He gave me a mention in his speech too, which made me cry. It was such a lovely moment and really emotional. He made everyone laugh by talking about how last time he was there it was 'a right nutty night' and he 'ended up licking Mary Berry'. Then he said, 'I like to think I won this award for being a blinding actor but it's probably because my daughter Dani won *Love Island*!' Jack was there with us and it was amazing because the press were asking all of us questions together rather than just me watching Dad

from the sidelines. But it was definitely Dad's night. He is the best actor out there in my eyes.

If he wasn't an actor, I reckon Dad should try his hand in politics. When I was in *Love Island* he made the headlines because he was on this show called *Good Evening Britain* with Piers Morgan and started ranting about Brexit and how it's a load of rubbish. He was applauded by all these newspapers for speaking the mind of the nation! The *Guardian* wrote, 'Who will speak for England in its moment of crisis? The answer this summer, it appears, is actor Danny Dyer, who – with a bit of help from his daughter Dani – is dominating the national conversation.'

Dad might have made people laugh by what he said – 'Who knows about Brexit? No one has got a fucking clue what Brexit is!' – but he actually knows what he's talking about. He's always watching stuff like *Newsnight* and ranting at the TV. He'll only give an opinion if he's informed about something, even if it does just sound funny to everyone else. The best bit on the show was when he was ranting about the old prime Minister David Cameron. 'What's happened to that twat Cameron who brought it on? How come he can scuttle off? He called all this on. Where is he? He's in Europe, in Nice with his trotters up. Where is the geezer? I think he should be held accountable for it.'

He won 'TV moment of the year' at the Edinburgh TV Festival for that rant and he couldn't believe it. But my dad's always been very, very honest and he's true to his heart. He says what everyone else is thinking – stuff that no one else will dare speak out loud.

I think he should go for PM himself one day. I quite fancy putting my own trotters up in Number 10. I think he'd be a good prime minister because he's normal and a proper representative of real people. If Dad was PM, we would live in a very free, equal world. He'd definitely focus on equality more – we talk about how men and women are equal but we're not treated that way. Just because we're saying it, doesn't mean we're doing it.

'My dad would make a great prime minister. It would be a very free world if he ran the country!'

What Would Dani Do?

♡

What's next for you? What's your dream job?

@Lucy_Sumners

Lucy, 19, South London

Being completely honest, despite all the amazing opportunities I've been getting with TV work, and my clothing range, it's acting that I miss the most. It's what

I really want to do and always has been. I went to a big ITV event and they showed a trailer of all the new dramas they have coming up for the next year and as I watched them I just thought, 'That's what I call talent. I want that to be me.' I'd love to do something like Our Girl so that's my aim. I'm going to loads of auditions, and I have some really exciting meetings lined up so watch this space!

(Saying that, if Strictly Come Dancing want to give me a call I'd also be happy to be whisked around the dance floor. The only thing I'd be worried about would be the curse – so be warned, Jack!)

What Would Dani Do?

What would you do if you won the lottery?

That's a hard one! You know what, I think I would set up an old people's centre and make it really sociable with a massive restaurant so they never have to eat alone.

Chapter Twelve

What Dani Did Next

Jack and I filmed a reality show for ITVBe called *Jack and Dani: Life after Love Island,* in which the cameras followed us round to capture what we'd got up to since winning the show. I was worried people wouldn't want to watch it and might have got bored of us, but, to my relief, the viewing figures were really good! We had to squeeze filming in around all the other commitments we had, and I'm not going to lie, there were times when it was tough to do because we were either really tired or we'd had a row beforehand. But we tried to be really honest and talk openly about the stuff we were going through on camera, which hopefully reminded people why they voted for us to win in the first place.

For the end of the series we were flown to China, which should have been an incredible experience if only we hadn't stupidly decided to go out on a massive bender the night before the flight, meaning I had zero sleep and I proceeded to not sleep for the whole four days because of the jetlag! This screwed with my head so badly and I was in floods of tears every day, telling Jack I couldn't cope. It was such a surreal location to be in and I felt so out of place and far away from home. It didn't help that I had to do a poo in a hole on the floor while I was there (talk about saying goodbye to your dignity!).

I felt bad for the poor camera crew who had to put up with me, but Jack was incredible, and I don't think I'd have coped without him. My anxiety had kicked in again and he totally supported me and remained really strong and calm throughout. When I watched that episode back I was worried that I would come across as a moody mess but somehow I didn't. Although I felt out of my comfort zone the scene where Jack and I are in a restaurant is actually quite funny because we are nearly being sick at the sight of the food coming out – everything had eyes and heads! All I wanted was chicken and noodles – not to see the whole bird! In the end I just drank the beer. At least that didn't have a face.

Behind the scenes, by the end of 2018, things between me and Jack were really getting bad. We were bickering daily about anything and everything, and it was tough. I was thinking, 'What are we arguing for? Is this all we have left?' Jack loves going out and I felt like all I was doing was moaning at him. There was no way I thought he would ever cheat on me, though, that didn't come into the equation. But because we were living together, I would be at home lying in bed, tossing and turning and I wouldn't be able to sleep.

Looking back, I think the main problem was that I put him on such a pedestal in *Love Island*, it was as if he was this mythical creature – and no human being could possibly live up to that. In the villa he was so kind to me, he adored me and treated me like a princess, then when we came out of the show and moved in together we were obsessed with each other. But the honeymoon had to end at some point and we had to deal with normal life. And normal life brings with it stupid arguments and other niggles. I would say, 'The Jack I met wouldn't have done that', but that wasn't fair because he was still the Jack I met on the show – he just didn't have any outside influences then. We both had to face facts: we were real human beings with flaws and nothing about either of us was perfect. Jack has a very sensitive and beautiful and loving side but then there's also a side that is all about 'my mates, my mates!', and I'm sure Jack would say that while I have a very kind and caring side, I also have a very bitchy angry side!

But the whole thing was getting to me. I was crying loads, I wasn't feeling like myself, I wasn't enjoying it any more. I didn't want to be screaming at my boyfriend every day. I'd been that girl before and I didn't want to make myself ill again. My best mate Kayleigh was telling me, 'It's not making you happy so something needs to change.'

But the problem was that I still loved him and I couldn't imagine being with anyone else. I was worried I was giving up too soon. I'd met Jack in this bubble and I didn't want that bubble to pop.

It all came to a head in early December. We actually split a couple of times briefly before the press got hold of the story, but it was in the heat of the moment after an argument and I'd say, 'I can't do this any more', and then we wouldn't speak for a day. Then I would get back from work and Jack would do something to make me laugh so we would gloss over the row without dealing with the issues.

Crunch time finally came on the day we did a joint interview for *Heat* magazine's Christmas issue. We sat talking to the journalist about our relationship and making jokes but deep down we couldn't stand each other – and that wasn't right. Immediately after the shoot we ended up having another full-blown argument and that's when I knew it was done. I was the one to end things because I couldn't see any other way.

I didn't expect it to go public as soon as it did, but somehow the story leaked to the press and within seconds everyone was talking about it. Our PRs told us we should make a statement so we both agreed the wording and said we would put it on our Instagram accounts at the same time that night. It was around 8 p.m., when, sat on the sofa at my mum and dad's house, I posted it on my Instagram stories; 'Jack and I have sadly decided to part ways. It's been an incredible six months, and we will always have a place in our hearts for each other, but sadly we've come to the realisation that it's not meant to be long term. We both plan to stay friends. Hope you'll all understand. Love Dani x'

My mum looked at me. 'Dani – why have you just posted that on Instagram?'

We'd both agreed to do it, I told her. But half an hour went by and Jack still hadn't put anything up on his Instagram account. I messaged him: 'Why haven't you put up the statement?', and he replied that he didn't want us to split and he thought if he didn't post it, then it might mean we could get back together.

The next day there was an 'exclusive' article in the *Sun* saying how heartbroken he was over it all. I looked like a heartless bitch who had ended it while he was all innocent. I was convinced his PR had placed the story, although Jack assured me that wasn't the case. But from then on I felt like the press and all our followers had turned against me – I was made out to be this horrible person who didn't have any feelings. A few days after that, someone recorded a chat with Jack in a pub saying that I had dumped him for publicity. Jack was drunk and pissed off and had been ranting nonsense not thinking about what he was saying. He certainly didn't think it would be in the paper the next day.

So the comments got worse and people were properly hating on me. People said I was a ruthless cow and just cared about my career. It upset me so much, I couldn't stop crying. I thought, 'I'm none of the things they're saying I am. I broke up with my boyfriend. The guy I loved and still do. Not because of business but because it wasn't working and I was unhappy.' No one knew what had really gone on behind closed doors.

Nearly a week had gone by and I felt so miserable. I still loved Jack but I didn't like the person I'd become when I was with him. He said he would change and that we could make it work. In the end it was my dad who convinced me to try again. He saw things from Jack's point of view – he's been there, done that – and he knows what boys are like. He sat me down and asked, 'Dani, do you think you've made the right decision? You've both gone through a lot together and all in the public eye. You did have something special.

You might regret it if you don't try again. Don't you think you should give him another chance?'

So, we agreed to meet. I had been staying at Mum and Dad's so I picked him up from the pub and we drove back to the flat to talk. We had a heart-to-heart and I told him how I was feeling – I said we needed to become more of a team and not be so separate. We decided we need to stop putting so many labels on things and just enjoy what we have without all the pressure.

So that's what we've been doing. Jack has really made an effort and has changed in certain aspects. He will never *not* be a party boy but I feel like he's respecting me more and we are making time to do stuff together. I won't pretend it's easy but we both want it to work and we know we have a lot of love for each other. We're still learning and we know that's alright. I know he is 100% faithful; I know he loves me and I love him. We get on so well and when things are good we laugh so hard, it's just brilliant. But I hate arguing and I don't ever want the rows to outweigh the laughs. I don't want it to get toxic.

Once we'd decided to make another go of it I felt relieved and happy. It did upset me a bit that some people said I'd just got back with Jack because of the negative press, but my dad told me I have to stop listening so much to other people and instead focus on what matters to me and Jack.

After that, we were suddenly into the whirlwind of Christmas and I was working non-stop in *Nativity!* with Dad, so I didn't get to see Jack as much as I'd have liked. But I went over to his mum's house on Christmas night and we swapped presents – Jack bought me a ring (not *that* kind!), some running trainers and a bag, and I got him a Prada coat, some Reiss tops and smelly stuff he likes. It felt so nice being boyfriend and girlfriend again. Sometimes I think that splitting up can jolt people into realising what they have, and you just get stronger because of it.

We went on holiday together at the start of January and it was exactly what we needed. We flew to Dubai on New Year's Day and had the best time. We just lazed about, ate nice food, got pissed and danced about (although Jack posted an Instagram story of me drunk on the beach, which didn't go down well with my dad!). We were lucky enough to have been offered a free trip in exchange for posting a competition about the hotel and company that flew us there, which was just the nuts. (There was a ridiculous rumour that we'd been paid 40k to go on holiday, which was *not* true – I wish!)

Back home, the lease on the flat we shared was up for renewal in February, and we both agreed it felt too small and we wanted to move. The problem was, we couldn't agree on the location – Jack wanted to be in South London, and I wanted to go back to Essex.

In the end, after a lot of debate, we took the 'grown up' decision to get separate places. I struggled with it at first, because I was worried it meant we were taking a massive step backwards, but the sensible side of me knew it would be better for us long-term because we are both still young. It would mean that when we did see each other, it would be quality time rather than just bickering over dinner and cleaning. So, Jack is getting his own place and I moved into a cute little house with a garden thirty minutes away from my family and friends. I was so excited about making it my own and being able to decorate it all just as I wanted. Jack kept the dog, but that was always going to be the case because she was his baby. And we both agreed to block time out of our diaries to do things together like going to the cinema or for a Sunday roast – nothing fancy, just doing what proper couples do.

Work wise, things were going really well. Performing in *Nativity!* was so much fun – even though we only got one day off over Christmas, I loved it so much. Working with my dad was brilliant; I never knew I could get on with someone so much in my life. We are like best mates and having that time together was really special. I used to love making him jump, so I would sneak into his dressing room while he was outside having a cigarette and hide in his cupboards or wardrobe or under his dressing table. Sometimes, I would be squashed in a place for ages waiting for him to come back, but it was worth it to see his face, scared out of his wits! It makes me laugh just thinking about it now. I don't know how I managed to shock him every time, but he would literally be in the air! He'd say, 'What are you doing to me? That ain't right! Karma is going to get you back one day!' It was so funny. The cast of *Nativity!* were so welcoming too. They made the whole experience wonderful. They'd been performing it around the country and we only joined for the last leg, but everyone was so kind to us and supportive. When I felt nervous on the first day, I knew as I stepped onto the stage that they all had my back and that meant a lot. The buzz and adrenaline I got after each performance was something else. I will never forget it as long as I live.

Jack and I had the opportunity to present backstage at the National Television Awards at the start of the year, which was another amazing opportunity and something we are still pinching ourselves about now. Then, I was asked by Comic Relief if I wanted to climb Mount Kilimanjaro. Wow, what an honour. One of my mates told me it would be just like climbing a hill, which made me laugh – it was going to take us eight days and it can be really dangerous! When Fearne Cotton did it a few years ago, she suffered really badly with altitude sickness – she got a nosebleed and collapsed – so I know I have to take the training really seriously and that just going to the gym a few days a week isn't going to cut it! At the time of pressing 'print' on this book I haven't yet done the climb but I'm really excited about the people I'm going to be doing it with – especially Jade and Leigh-Anne from Little Mix. Also joining us are the actor and presenter Alexander Armstrong, the policitican Ed Balls, presenter Dan Walker and Shirley Ballas from *Strictly Come Dancing*. A really interesting mix of people. A few days before the trip I am due to fly out to Freetown in Sierra Leone to visit some of the areas that Comic Relief helps, and I know it will be a life-changing experience. I also know I will get really angry seeing the kids, because there are kids with iPads in the UK but over there some children can't even get a bottle of water; it's just totally unfair.

And that's why it's so important that I do it. For all the exciting things I have been able to do since *Love Island* – like my clothing range, my eyelashes and hair and skincare deals – it's doing something like this that really matters. I want to make a difference. I will never let myself forget that I'm in a really privileged position, and if I can make other people's lives better in some way, then I'll feel like I've done my bit.

AND FINALLY . . .

I know I'm still young but I feel like I've learnt so much about myself and what makes me happy and sad and how to deal with situations that aren't good for me. I'm a much better person now than I've ever been, and I'm definitely stronger. I know the importance of waking up every morning and being in a positive mindset. Life is about the energy you put into it, and when you think good thoughts, you can make good stuff happen. I genuinely can't believe the incredible things that have happened to me in the last 12 months and I can't wait to see what's around the corner. I'm so grateful for every opportunity that's come my way and for those who have supported me. But I know that no matter what happens, it's so important to stay as grounded and as normal as possible. Thankfully, with a mum and dad like mine, there's no way I can be anything else.

If I ever get too up myself, I will soon know about it!

I hope this book has made you realise that I still struggle with insecurities and worries the same as you. At the end of the day, we are all still human no matter what we do, what we look like or how we might appear – everyone has feelings and everyone has issues. And you have to remember it's OK not to be OK sometimes. Don't be ashamed of anything. My life has been up and down so much but the thing about that is when you have downs you always have an up — and that's what you should hang on to. I believe if we all stick together and all support each other then it will make everything a little bit easier.

So let's look out for one another and take time to be kind.

SOME THINGS I KNOW NOW

- How to be a really good mate

- Not to listen to the trolls and to stand your ground and be honest and true to yourself

- Not to care so much what others think of you

- You need to compromise in a relationship (and get a cleaner to save arguments!)

- Your mum and dad are always your best judges

- Having a nose that looks like a carrot is what makes you unique

- Never put hair removal cream on your top lip before a big red–carpet event

- Always be kind to old people

- Don't be ashamed of going to therapy

- Justin Bieber is never going to marry you

- Keira Knightley is a great babysitter

- You are allowed to have some 'me time' – it's not always good for you if you're just trying to keep everyone else happy

- *The Secret* is a good book after all

- So is this one . . . (so tell your mates!)

SOME STUFF I STILL NEED ANSWERS TO

- Why do hangovers hurt so much?

- Why can't Internet trolls be banned?

- When will my dad become PM?

- When will Hollywood come calling?

- Why the hell haven't *Vogue* got back to me?!

- When will they put sugar back in Tango Ice Blasts?

- When will they make a bigger Cadbury Creme Egg? I love a Creme Egg with a cup of tea.

Acknowledgements

Huge thanks to Lucie Cave for being an amazing ghostwriter, and to Michelle Warner and all the lovely girls at Ebury for being so supportive on this project and making a book I'm really really proud of.

Mum and Dad, thank you for everything you've ever done for me. The support, the guidance, the constant love and always making me feel good about myself. You are both truly one in a million and I feel so lucky to have you. You have made me the person I am today.

To my little sister Dun Duns and Arty – watching you grow every day into such beautiful human beings makes me so happy. I love you both and I promise to try and guide you in all the right ways I possibly can.

Nanny and Bruv, I love you both so much. You are both my everything and I can't imagine my life without you. The way you can drink a Bacardi, Nan, and the way you can cook a paella, Bruv, is something I don't think I'll ever be able to accomplish.

Uncle Tolo thank you for putting me through my paces with training for half marathons and making sure I complete them. I have never known someone to be able to put a whole roast potato in their mouth, and to have so many jobs and still fit time in for training. I love you.

Sue – for always being in my life since I was a baby. You taught me how to sing 'Lollipop' and thank you for letting me torture you with my hate for nursery. You are such a beautiful kind soul and I really love how good you are at cleaning a shower door.

Adam, Dana, Caroline and the rest of the Money Management team. Thank you for EVERYTHING you do for me. You ⸺ friends for life and I feel blessed every day to have such amazing management who have stuck by me, helping me become successful and given me the best I could have. I adore you all so much.

Marcos . . . BEAUTIFUL inside and out. You are one of the kindest souls and I honestly do love ya. You're not only my stylist, you're a friend who I can confide in and I thank you so much for that.

To Lewis Evans for giving me the fantastic opportunity of *Love Island* (after dislocating my shoulder on *Survival of the Fittest*, you owed me one), and all the ITV grown-ups Lauren Benson, Richard Cowles, Angela Jain and Paul Mortimer. I know I've given you all grey hairs, but I love you!

To my *Love Island* girls and boys: Georgia, Samira, Laura, Josh, Kaz, Dr Alex, Wes, Megan, Alexandra and every bloody one of you. What a journey we had.

Roman Kemp, Vick Hope, Sonny Jay, Joe Lyons, Paul Phelps, Brent Tobin and the rest of the team at Capital Breakfast. You make getting up early so much fun!

Adam, Jamie and everyone at In The Style, thank you so much for the opportunity of helping me bring out my own fashion range. I had no idea how much of a success it would be and I am so glad I have met friends for life. Hollie, you taught me how to 'sell it with my eyes' haha! I love you, girl. Nothing makes me happier than trying on my clothes with you.

Jack, my handsome boy. Thank you for everything. You taught me how to really love and care for someone again and you gave me the most Disney romantic summer. You are one of the funniest people I have ever met and we have shared an experience that can never be taken from us. I love you millions. You are someone I am so glad to have met.

To my beautiful friends. Especially my best ones, Kayleigh, Ellie, Charlotte, Daisy and Liv. I love and adore you girls with all my heart. Thank you for always supporting me and letting me be Dani. You have gone through the worst and the best moments with me and have always managed to pick me up and make me laugh again. I love you so so much! It's very rare to find what I have with you girls in a friendship.

And finally to all my fans, a huge thank you for all your love and support. You put a massive smile on my face, and I feel so grateful that you've taken me into your hearts. Love you all! xx

Picture Credits